KENYA

For Angela

ACKNOWLEDGEMENTS

To Patrick Leparleen for information on the Samburu people and Peter Davey for help on the location of Kenya's bird life.

Dennis Lakin was born in London but has lived all his adult life in Kenya. He served in the Colonial Service from 1953 until Kenya's independence in 1963 and then served the new government for a further two years. After joining the tourist industry as East Africa manager for the largest tour operator, he started the Aga Khan's innovative hotel venture in the three East African countries, subsequently opening his own tourism related consultancy firm. Lakin has written a *Guide and Manual to Kenya* specifically aimed at the travel industry and many articles for magazines and journals related to tourism. He currently heads a hotel management company involved in developing a chain of up-market tented game lodges.

KENYA

Dennis Lakin

PASSPORT BOOKS
a division of *NTC Publishing Group*
Lincolnwood, Illinois USA

Published by Passport Books in conjunction with
The Guidebook Company Ltd

This edition was first published in 1992 by Passport Books,
a division of NTC Publishing Group, 4255 W Touhy Avenue
Lincolnwood (Chicago), Illinois 606-46-1975 U S A
originally published by The Guidebook Company Ltd
© 1992 The Guidebook Company Ltd. All rights reserved.
Library of Congress Catalog Card Number: 92-60495

Grateful acknowledgement is made to the following authors and publishers for
permissions granted:

E P Dutton (an imprint of New American Library, a division of Penguin Books USA Inc) for
Petals of Blood © 1977 by Ngugi wa Thiong'o

David Higham Associates for
Happy Valley: The Story of the English in Kenya © 1979 by Nicholas Best

Faber & Faber Ltd for
East African Journey © 1976 by Margery Perham

Leo Cooper, Pen & Sword Books Ltd for
My African Journey by Winston Churchill © Leo Cooper 1989

Charles Scribner's Sons, New York for
African Game Trails © 1910 by Theodore Roosevelt

Random Century Ltd and Chatto & Windus for
The Flame Trees of Thika by Elspeth Huxley © 1959

Contributing Editor: Nigel Sitwell
Series Editors: David Clive Price and Caroline Robertson
Illustrations Editor: Caroline Robertson
Design: U Wang Graphics
Map Design: Bai Yiliang

Front cover (clockwise):
Alan Binks; Michael Mong; Angela Fisher/Robert Estall Photographs; Nigel R Pavitt

Photography supplied courtesy of Alan Binks 8-9, 84-5, 117, 124-5, 129, 153, 162, 166, 171 (below),
185, 204-5; Angela Fisher/Robert Estall Photographs 5, 43-46, 96, 200; Bill Hurst 17 (above), 71, 81
(above), 89 (below), 156 (below left); Carol Beckwith/Robert Estall Photographs 201; Caroline Robertson 144-5, 156 (above); David Coulson/Robert Estall Photographs 98, 175, 180; Jon Resnick 60, 70, 93,
167, 196; Kenya National Archives, Nairobi 29, 33, 41, 54, 139, 165, 169, 171 (above); Nigel R Pavitt
24, 61, 64, 102, 106, 132-3, 188; Michael Mong 16, 17 (below), 21, 48, 57, 75, 81 (below), 89 (above),
103, 113, 116, 121, 132 (below), 133 (above and below right), 140, 141, 148, 156 (below right), 157,
193

Produced by Twin Age Limited, Hong Kong
Printed in Hong Kong by Sing Cheong Printing Co Ltd

The elaborate hairstyles of Samburu warriors belie their fearsome spirit

Contents

Star of Africa

The Republic of Kenya straddles the Equator, indeed is almost bisected by it. Its land area of 582,644 square kilometres (224,900 square miles), about the size of France, is bordered by five nations—Tanzania to the south, Uganda to the west, Sudan and Ethiopia to the north, and Somalia in the east. Within its borders lie almost every known land form: mountain massifs and rich savannahs, glacial ice and true desert, dense jungle and sparkling lakes, rich farmland, white sandy beaches and steaming volcanoes.

These variations of terrain are matched by extreme contrasts in climate caused mainly by altitude. The hot and often humid coastal climate gives way to the sparkling sunshine and bracing air of the highlands as the land rises from sea level to 2,000 metres (6,600 feet). The Highlands, in colonial days called 'the White Highlands', is an area of rich agricultural land and dense forest. The principal cash crops grown here are coffee, tea, pyrethrum and maize, combining to form an intricate mosaic of shades of green.

The Great Rift Valley, one of the world's best-known geophysical features, is seen at its best in Kenya. Eight lakes, some fresh and some alkaline, glisten on the valley floor and one of these—Lake Turkana, the Jade Sea—is a favoured destination of the intrepid and the adventurous.

Another of the country's geophysical landmarks is the vast arid and semi-arid desert of Kenya's northern region, which occupies more than 200,000 square kilometres (77,000 square miles), more than one third of the country's land area.

And then there is the Indian Ocean littoral, 480 kilometres (300 miles) in length with long stretches of idyllic, silver-sanded beaches fringed by waving palms.

Between the coast and the highlands is a seemingly endless tract of bush and savannah, in which lie three of Kenya's most famous national parks—Tsavo West, Tsavo East, and Amboseli. All three parks lie close to Africa's highest mountain, Kilimanjaro, whose majestic, snow-capped cone soars 5,900 metres (19,340 feet) into the azure sky.

This, then, is Kenya, a land endowed by nature with breathtaking beauty, extraordinary variety and a close to perfect climate. Within this bounty lie other, perhaps more tangible attractions. There are over 50 national parks and reserves affording sanctuary to over 100 species of mammals and 1,200 species of birds. These sanctuaries occupy about eight per cent of Kenya, or a land area about the size of Switzerland. No one park is a replica of another, for they differ in variety and abundance of game, in climate and in altitude. Not to be overlooked are the coastal resorts—some elegant and sophisticated, and some so remote as to attract the traveller rather than the tour-

(preceding pages) *Mount Kenya*

ist. The entire coastline is fringed with reefs, making swimming totally safe and offering visitors the opportunity to enjoy the riches of the underwater world.

Finally, there is the wilderness, strangely magnetic to the adventurous and the inquisitive. Here visitors find not only solitude but people and cultures quite different from their own—nomadic people whose simple lifestyles contrast starkly with Western values. And in the remotest corner of the land is the place where man began: the cradle of mankind.

Getting To Kenya

The majority of visitors arrive by air, with more than 30 airlines serving Nairobi's Jomo Kenyatta International airport, some 17 kilometres (11 miles) from the city centre. Kenya Airways, the national airline, flies daily to and from London; on some flights stops are made in other European capitals. Several European carriers fly more than three times a week and although most flights are overnight there are also a few daylight ones. There are currently no American carriers flying to Kenya. Visitors from the Far East and from Australia also have to make a flight change and possibly a stopover en route.

A considerable number of charters fly direct from Europe to Moi International airport at Mombasa, although the only scheduled carrier currently using this destination is Kenya Airways.

If you have plenty of time, and a diligent travel agent, it might be possible to find a berth on a cargo ship travelling to Mombasa. The first of these considerations is definitely necessary for those choosing to sail from the Gulf or Pakistan on the *dhows* that visit Kenya from October through March, blown by the winds of the northeast monsoon.

Alternatively, with adequate time on your hands and a strong back, you can take one of the overland trips from Europe. Details of some of these operations can be found on page 18.

All visitors to Kenya require a valid passport and some may require visas. Visitors arriving from, or who have passed through, certain countries may require particular innoculations. More details of visa and health requirements are given on pages 22-25.

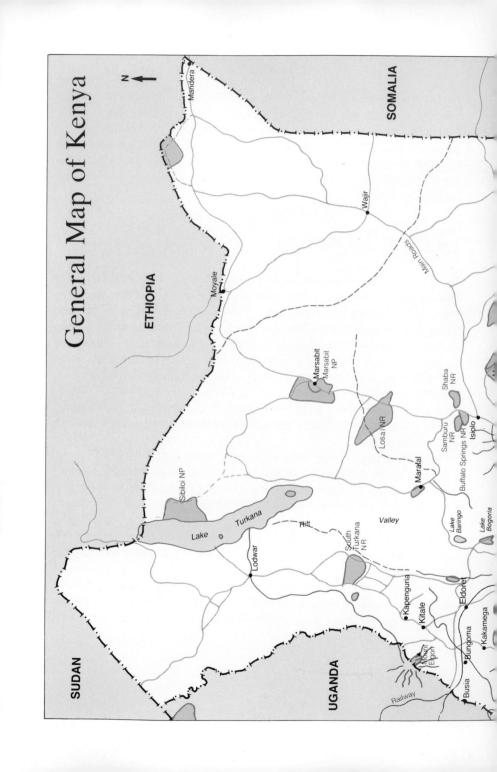

General Map of Kenya

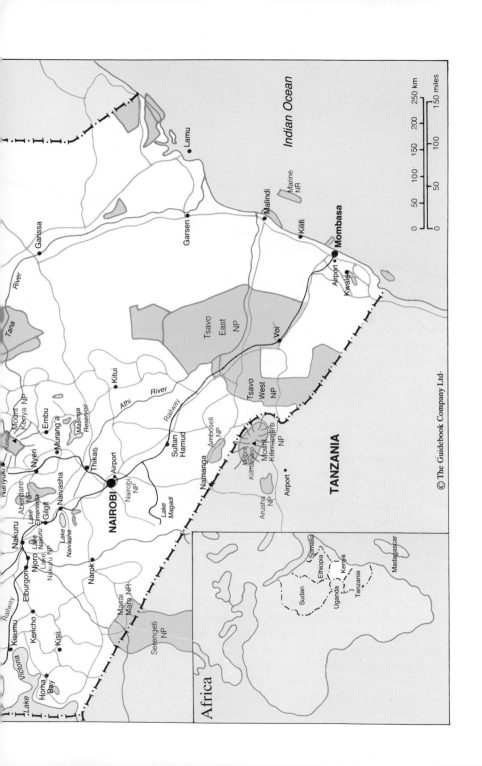

Indian Ocean

• Lamu

Malindi
Marine NR

Garsen • Kilifi

Mombasa
Airport
Kwale

Tsavo East NP

Voi

Tsavo West NP

Kitui

Athi   River

Railway

Amboseli NP

Sultan Hamud

Namanga

Mount Kilimanjaro NP
Mount Kilimanjaro

Airport •

Arusha NP

TANZANIA

Ganissa

Tana River

Tana

Mount Kenya NP
Mount Kenya

Embu •
Murang'a •

Nyeri •

Masinga Reservoir

Thika •

Airport
NAIROBI
Nairobi NP

Lake Magadi

Naivasha •
Gilgit •

Lake Elementeita
Lake Naivasha

Nakuru

Njoro •
Lake Nakuru NP
Lake Nakuru

Elburgon •

Narok •

Masai Mara NR

Serengeti NP

Nanyuki

Kenya

Aberdare NP
Lake

Railway

Kisumu •
Kericho •
Kisii •

Lake Victoria

Homa Bay •

Lake

0   50   100   150   200   250 km

0   50   100   150 miles

© The Guidebook Company Ltd·

Africa

Sudan

Ethiopia
Somalia

Uganda
Kenya

Tanzania

Madagascar

Facts For The Traveller

Getting Around

Visitors who wish to see the wildlife sanctuaries will almost certainly join a tour.
Arrangements can be made in your own country or on arrival in Kenya. If the tour is
bought overseas it will probably include accommodation at the beginning and at the
end in a Nairobi or a coast hotel. Some recommended tour operators are listed on
page 18. It can be risky to delay reservations until you arrive, especially in the high
seasons (Christmas to Easter, and the month of August) and even at other times of
the year. So if you have definite ideas about what you want to see and where you
want to go, you should make plans well in advance.

There are, however, usually a large selection of tours on offer from any one of
several hundred tour operators plying out of Nairobi or Mombasa, so that even if you
arrive with no prior arrangements it will always be possible to pick up some kind of
tour, albeit not necessarily the one you would most prefer.

Itineraries covering the game parks are generally carefully worked out to ensure
the minimum of backtracking and the maximum time in the parks, but if you are
coming to look at wildlife then choose a tour that gives you the most time to do just
that. Count the number of 'game drives' that the tour operator says he will be giving
you, as those matter much more than either the route or the accommodation.

You can, of course, arrange a tailor-made tour either through an overseas tour
operator or when you arrive in Kenya, or by communicating direct with a Kenyan
operator. Such tours are more expensive than joining with other visitors in a group
but they have the definite advantage of enabling you to choose both your route and
your company.

Whichever way you take a tour you will be driven and escorted by a Kenyan
driver-guide. This man may make or break a tour; not only does he need to be an
expert driver but he is also your companion and mentor. The best driver-guides are
retained by the best companies.

Almost all tour operators use nine-seater minibuses. These are custom-built for
the job and all have roof hatches from which photography is made easy. Check how
many passengers your tour operator will put in a bus, as two of the nine seats are not
adjacent to windows. You will find that the best companies do not put more than
seven passengers in a nine-seater vehicle. This not only makes for better game-viewing but also gives you some room to scatter your possessions. Since vehicle costs are a
major component of the tour price, it follows that if you want a budget tour you will
have to put up with a greater number of passengers per bus.

You can decide to drive yourself: Hertz, Avis, and Europcar are all represented, and there are very many local car-hire firms. Driving is on the left. But self-drive has its drawbacks, not least of which is the poor state of the Kenyan roads and an unrivalled ignorance of the Highway Code by many Kenyan drivers. Road signs tend to be few and far between. Another major snag arises in the parks, where having to drive frustrates many a fine photographer. There are very few companies offering minibuses on a self-drive basis, and for game-viewing either a minibus or a four-wheel drive vehicle with a roof hatch is essential. Avoid saloon cars, which are too low-slung for the park roads and also too low, particularly when the grass is long, for good photographic opportunities.

There are daily scheduled flights by light aircraft to the Masai Mara, Samburu, and Amboseli, and at these destinations you can buy game drives in vehicles stationed at the lodges. So if these parks are on your itinerary you may find that this the best way to get around. Certainly there is little wasted time and undoubtedly flying is more comfortable, but some visitors believe they lose contact with the scenery and the people. Many tour operators offer total or partial air safaris; in the latter, aircraft are used to cover long and sometimes tedious sectors.

If you have nerves of steel and can therefore cope with the fast speeds and the daredevil attitude of the local drivers you can get around the country quite well, and very cheaply, by *matatu* or by bus. *Matatus* (the Kenya equivalent of the Israeli *sherut*) are small vehicles, usually so packed that the conductor has to hang onto the outside. To Kenyans, travel by *matatu* is a way of life; to most foreigners it must be the last resort. However, there is no public transport in the national parks and reserves so even if you can get as far as the gate (itself quite a task) you will not be able to ride around inside the park. Visitors who have paid for a tour are usually unwilling to offer lifts. Between the main centres, Nairobi to Mombasa for instance, there are better and safer coaches available, so that method of travel should not be ruled out. Hitching lifts anywhere in the country is difficult and no visitor should contemplate following a fixed itinerary by that means.

Kenya Railways operate an efficient overnight service in both directions between Nairobi and Mombasa. Passengers board in the evening, have dinner, and then retire to comfortable sleeping cars to awake in time for breakfast and arrival shortly afterwards. The slower of the two evening trains stops rather frequently (some say 43 times) so it is best to book the express! This is not the fastest way to or from the coast but definitely one to be tried, at least in one direction. There is also a sleeper service to and from Kisumu on Lake Victoria, and although there are other routes, the slowness of the trains and their infrequency makes them unlikely to be of much value to a visitor.

Leopard, Masai Mara

Zebras, Amboseli (above);
Flamingos, Lake Bogoria (left)

The national airline, Kenya Airways, operates domestic services to Mombasa, Malindi, and Kisumu, with most flights by Fokker F50 aircraft. A private operator, Air Kenya, also flies scheduled services to these destinations, although with less frequency. There is an airport service charge of Ksh 50 per passenger at all the major domestic airports. Several private air operators run scheduled air services to the three parks already mentioned and also to Lamu (both from Nairobi and Mombasa), Nanyuki, Nyeri, and Eldoret. If you stay at the coast you will find that coast tour operators offer 'packaged' private air charters and accommodation and offer all-inclusive air tours to the principal parks.

For the active, there are walking, horseback, and camel safaris available, all of which are packaged so that you buy a complete safari rather than just the use of a guide or an animal. The Kenya Association of Tour Operators, PO Box 48461, Nairobi, Fax No 254 2 218402 can supply you with a list of its members.

Some specialist tour operators who can be recommended are:

Birds and Birding	East African Ornithological Safaris, PO Box 48019, Nairobi
Camel Safaris	Ewaso River Camel Hikes, PO Box 109, Rumuruti
Bicycle Tours	Hiking and Biking (Kenya) Ltd, PO Box 39439, Nairobi
Horseback Safaris	Safaris Unlimited Ltd, PO Box 24181, Nairobi
Mountain Climbing	Tropical Ice Ltd, PO Box 57341, Nairobi

Accommodation

Nairobi has nine 5-star hotels, not all in the city centre, including representatives of the Hilton and Inter-Continental chains. Another five economy class hotels, acceptable to international travellers, can be found in the city centre and there are plenty of others in peripheral locations. There are no hotels of international standard in Mombasa town, although there are many in nearby beach locations. Mombasa has several economy class hotels.

Lodges, variously termed wildlife, game, or safari lodges, are actually small hotels, generally architecturally innovative and imaginatively decorated. The largest sleep no more than 200 people and the smallest around 30.

Tented camps in Kenya are a far cry from the boy scout concept of camping; some are in fact quite luxurious, including even four-poster beds, and all have flush toilet facilities. Private tented camps, on the other hand, are nearer to nature, partly because they are mobile and partly because the intention is that the guests experience a true safari atmosphere. Predictably, private tented safaris are the most expensive accommodation available.

In town hotels and lodges check-out time is usually 10 am and at most coast hotels 11 am. Many flights arrive in Nairobi in the early morning and if a room is essential on arrival it will be necessary to book for the preceding night.

Banking

All the larger towns have banks and each has a foreign currency counter or a *bureau de change*. The rate of exchange for the principal world currencies is set daily by the Central Bank of Kenya, so there is generally very little difference between one bank and another (there should be none!). The larger hotels and game lodges are also licensed to accept and exchange foreign currencies, but almost certainly the rate will be lower than in a bank. While on safari, there is little option but to exchange foreign currency at a game lodge as banks do not exist in the parks. The rate of exchange is always better for travellers' cheques than for cash.

Banks are open from 9 am to 2 pm, Monday through Friday, and from 9 am to 11 am on the first and last Saturday of each month. There is a 24–hour banking service at both Nairobi and Mombasa international airports.

Currency and currency regulations

Kenyan currency is based on the decimal system. The unit of currency is the shilling, divided into 100 cents. Coins are denominated in 5, 10, and 50 cents, 1 and 5 shillings, while notes are in denominations of 10, 20, 50,100, 200, and 500 shillings.

It is illegal to enter or leave Kenya with any Kenyan currency. If, when you are about to leave, you have a surplus of Kenyan currency you may change this back into a convertible currency at the airport bank. It is important to retain the paperwork that you are given when you change foreign currency. You are strongly advised to steer clear of people on the street offering to sell you Kenyan currency at a discount. It is an offence to destroy or deface Kenyan currency.

Customs

Used personal effects, still and cine cameras and video equipment, providing they are of a non-commercial nature, are temporarily allowed entry free of customs duty. Refundable deposits may be required for the temporary import of radios, tape recorders and musical instruments. Firearms can only be imported with an import permit issued in advance by the Central Firearms Bureau (PO Box 30263, Nairobi). The import of agricultural or horticultural produce is prohibited except by special permit.

Departure

An airport departure tax, US$20 at the time of writing, is payable on leaving Kenya. This tax must be paid in convertible currency and may not be paid in Kenyan shillings. There is a departure tax of Ksh 50 per person charged on leaving Nairobi, Mombasa, Malindi, and Kisumu airports on domestic flights.

There are duty free shops at both Jomo Kenyatta International and Moi International airports, and purchases there must be made in an acceptable foreign currency. Customs may require the inspection of outgoing luggage.

Note that all personal baggage is weighed before departure and the conventions regarding size, rather than weight of suitcases (which are in use in some countries), are not applicable in Kenya.

Dress

The accent is on informality, although some hotel dining rooms (and the Mount Kenya Safari Club at Nanyuki) insist on men wearing jackets and ties at dinner. If you like to conform you may find it more comfortable to wear a jacket at some of the better Nairobi restaurants.

Safari suits or some other light casual cotton clothing, preferably of a neutral colour, are the order of the day whilst on safari. Early mornings and evenings can be cool, so a warm sweater is advised. At the tree hotels it can be very cool and a warm coat is recommended. A hat and a scarf are useful protection against sun and dust. Most of the lodges and some of the tented camps have swimming pools, so it is a good idea to bring a bathing suit. Light footwear is more comfortable for the long car journeys and in any event there is very little opportunity on safari for much walking.

Nairobi market: a mass of fruit and vegetable stalls overlooked by curio shops

At the coast, the lightest of clothing is needed, and although in July or August a light jacket might be used for dining out of doors, a tie is never worn (except by hotel managers).

Driving

If you are planning to drive while in Kenya a valid driving licence from your home country is acceptable but in theory requires endorsement at the Road Transport Office, Nyati House, Kenyatta Avenue, Nairobi, or at Provincial Headquarters, Mombasa. But this rule seems to be overlooked both by visitors and the police. An international driving licence does not require endorsement, so that may be preferable. Driving is on the left.

Electricity

Mains electricity and electricity generated in the lodges is 240 volts AC. If you are bringing a video camera make sure that you have a suitable adaptor that can charge your batteries from this supply.

Health

Evidence of innoculation against yellow fever and cholera are advisable, although not mandatory except in some instances as, for example, for arrivals from the Far East (cholera) and Central America and South, Central and West Africa (yellow fever). Visitors likely to arrive in Kenya who may pass through yellow fever areas or areas requiring yellow fever innoculations should obtain innoculations in advance. As innoculation requirements sometimes change, it is advisable to check the current rules with a scheduled airline that flies into Kenya.

Malaria is endemic in Kenya and it is essential to take precautions against contracting it. Firstly, it is important to take a prophylactic drug. The African Medical Research Foundation (to which the Flying Doctors' Society is affiliated), having recently conducted research in both Kenya and Tanzania, states that the drug of choice is Paludrine. This drug (containing proguanil and made by ICI) has been available in many countries for many years but has yet to be cleared by the US Food and Drug

Administration. Americans should seek advice from their doctors on recommended drugs.

Paludrine is available in Kenya without prescription. The drug should be started the day before entry into a malaria zone and continued for at least 14 days after leaving. The adult dose is 200 mg (two tablets) per day, preferably with food. Children under 15 kg (33 lbs), half a tablet a day; under 30 kg (66 lbs) one tablet a day; and under 45 kg (100 lbs) one and a half tablets a day. However, no prophylactic drug regime is 100 per cent effective and is in any case no replacement for personal protection. The best defence is to avoid mosquitoes. If mosquito nets are provided, use them. Wear long clothing after dark and use cream or repellent sprays on the skin. Spray your bedroom with an insecticide before going to bed.

Early diagnosis and treatment of malaria results in a cure, so at the first suspicious sign of fever you should see your doctor and explain that you have been in a malaria area.

Stomach disorders are quite common among visitors. Outside Nairobi (where the tap water is quite safe) it is wiser to drink boiled or bottled water or any of the proprietary soft drinks that are manufactured in hygienic conditions. Never drink water from a tap while on safari.

The main towns have good hospital care and Nairobi has excellent specialists available. For a small fee you can become a member of the Flying Doctors' Society, which among other benefits will entitle an injured or seriously ill person to free emergency evacuation by air from any part of Kenya to Nairobi. You should, of course, arrange medical insurance before you leave home.

Pharmaceutical facilities are good and chemist shops (drug stores) can be found in all the main centres. However, anyone requiring special and continuing medication should bring sufficient quantities to last the visit.

The equatorial sun can be deceptive, especially at high altitudes, and even on an overcast day can burn. Precautions against over exposure are advised, particularly at the coast where reflection from water and the white sand magnifies the sun's intensity.

Snake bites and scorpion stings are extremely rare and should be considered a very remote hazard. Do not bathe in rivers or lakes because of the possibility of bilharzia.

Hotel Classification

The Hotel and Restaurants Authority classifies all hotels into one of four classes. These are town hotels, vacation hotels, lodges and tented camps. In each category

hotels are graded into 5-, 4-, 3-, 2- and 1-star(s), 5 stars being the highest. When awarding stars, consideration is given to all factors affecting the overall standard of the hotel, and in particular the structure of the buildings and the amenities provided in the public rooms, recreational facilities, and grounds; the standard of cleanliness throughout the hotel and the sanitary facilities provided; the manner in which food is stored, prepared, cooked, and served, and the quality of the food; the degree of comfort afforded, the quality of the equipment and furnishings, the proportion of bathrooms to the number of guest rooms, and the number of private bathrooms in proportion to the hotel.

Immigration

All visitors must have a valid passport. Visa requirements vary from time to time, so if you are in any doubt call the airline with which you intend to fly or the nearest Kenya Embassy, High Commission, or Tourist Office. At the time of writing, citizens of Commonwealth countries do not require visas, but there are some exceptions.

Public Holidays

1 January, Good Friday, Easter Monday, 1 May, 1 June, 10 October, 20 October, 12 December, and 25–26 December are all public holidays. When the designated date falls on a Sunday then the following day is a public holiday. The Muslim festival of *Idd-Ul-Fitr*, the date of which changes from year to year, is also a public holiday.

Festivals are few and generally of only local significance. An exception is the *Maulidi* celebrations that mark the end of the month of the Prophet's birth. The *Maulidi* at Lamu is the most impressive; several days of dancing and parades end with recitation of the *Maulidi* in the square in front of the Riyadah Mosque. All the town's population gather here together with thousands of pilgrims, for the Lamu *Maulidi* is the next best thing for those unable to make the pilgrimage to Mecca. The problem for non-Muslims who wish to attend is finding out the date. This varies from year to year and perhaps the best way is to contact the Curator of the Lamu Museum (PO Box 48, Lamu)

Security

Kenya is little different from many other tourist centres with regard to security.

Gerenuk derive their nourishment solely from acacia trees and shrubs

Money and valuables should not be left in hotel or lodge bedrooms, even in a locked suitcase. Visitors should not carry large sums of cash, and women in particular should be wary of handbag snatchers in the streets of Nairobi. Another hazard for women is the incidence of necklace snatching in the streets. Nairobi is not a 'Gucci-Pucci' city and jewellery should be left in the hotel safe.

As in all major cities, walking in unfamiliar surroundings at night is a risk and it is prudent to take a taxi to a restaurant if you are dining out.

Telephones and Telex

An efficient subscriber trunk dialling service (STD) exists for both domestic and international calls and for facsimile services. Direct dial telex is also available round the clock. The lodges are all connected to their head offices by radio, and also to the Post Office radio telephone system.

Tipping

A service charge of either 5 or 10 per cent is added to most hotel and restaurant bills and in such cases tipping is not necessary, except where you wish to show your appreciation of exceptional service. If you take a group tour you may find that the tour operator includes tipping, which is done by the tour guide. Where a service charge is not included, a tip of between 5 and 10 per cent of the bill is fair.

As a general rule, a tip of Ksh 50 per person per day would be usual for your driver-guide, paid at the end of your safari.

Climate

It is hard to be precise about Kenya's climate as temperatures, and to a lesser extent rainfall, depend on altitude. The general rules are as follows.

The coast is sunny and hot year-round apart from July and August, when it is often overcast and is warm rather than hot. It is humid throughout the year but more so in May, June, and November. The long rains peak in May and June and the short rains in November, although there is likely to be some rain in the months on either side of those periods. The rain falls mostly in the late afternoon and at night, so even in the rainy periods there is usually plenty of sun. Nevertheless, there can be some rain in every month of the year.

In the Highlands it is warm year-round but cooler in July and August, when it is overcast. The long rains fall in April, May and June and the short rains from mid-October to late December. In both rainy seasons most of the rain falls in the evening or at night and the days are often bright and sunny.

In Samburu, Tsavo, Meru, and Amboseli it is hot most of the year apart from the overcast months of July and August.

Cancellation Charges

All lodges and coast hotels charge cancellation fees on accommodation cancelled or reduced within 30 days of intended occupation. For cancellations between 30 and 20 days before noon on the date of accommodation, the fee is 10 per cent of the rate applicable per night cancelled. Between 19 and 10 days the rate is 25 per cent, and between nine and two days, 35 per cent. Cancellations within 48 hours are treated as a no-show and the full value of the accommodation is charged. Nairobi hotels do not charge until nine days before intended occupation, when the same rates as for the lodges and coast hotels apply.

History

It now seems certain that our ancestors—yours and mine—came from Kenya. On the shores of Lake Turkana, almost at the Ethiopian border, is the womb of mankind. Now just about as hostile a landscape as can be imagined, it was once a Garden of Eden, a lush forest teeming with wildlife. About three million years ago a hominid stood erect and stayed that way. He was not of course '1470', the prosaic description for the fossil skull found by Bernard Ngeneo in 1972. But that find paved the way for other discoveries and for the now accepted theory that the first truly man-like creature hailed from the Lake Turkana area. The continuity of human evolution is attested by many other finds in eastern Africa. The late Dr Louis Leakey, his wife Mary, and their son Richard (now Director of Kenya's Wildlife Service) have spent their lifetimes exploring, exposing, and explaining the fossilized evidence of man's ancestry.

Although it is the best known of the hominid finds at Lake Turkana, '1470' is but one of several hundred in the same area that have contributed to our knowledge of man's origins. Nor was it the first *Homo* skull to be found, for Dr Louis Leakey had identified and named *Homo habilis* at Olduvai Gorge in Tanzania some ten years earlier.

The fragmentary evidence is far from complete, but the progression from *Homo habilis* to *Homo erectus* and thence to *Homo sapiens* is is a potential evolution strongly suggested by these discoveries. Visitors with advance permission from the National Museum of Kenya can visit Koobi Fora, a sand spit in Lake Turkana that is the base for this massive, on-going fossil hunt.

Fossil evidence of this period is supplemented by huge natural repositories of Stone Age artefacts, especially carefully crafted hand-axes and cleavers. A hunter's camp at Olorgesailie, 65 kilometres (40 miles) from Nairobi, has been excavated and left intact to show visitors this significant find, and perhaps the world's richest example of Acheulian hand-axe culture. Evidence such as this suggests the very definite possibility that the Stone Age progeny of *Homo erectus* emerged as hunters and gatherers, represented today by the **Boni** and **Sanye** peoples living north of the Tana River towards the border with Somalia. Despite subsequent invasions by pastoralists and cultivators, these people retained their way of life and, to a lesser extent, still do so today.

The first of these invasions occurred around 3,000 years ago, when Cushitic-speaking pastoralists entered Kenya from the north bringing with them cattle and a new economic freedom; the ownership of domestic stock freed man from the need to hunt. By living off the products of live animals, particularly blood and milk, they could expand their herds and so create a wealth economy.

By the second millennium BC, the Southern Cushitic-speaking people had occupied a large part of what is now Kenya and advanced farther south into Tanzania, absorbing the hunter-gatherer communities in the process. Some of their customs such as circumcision, both male and female, have endured and been accepted by other immigrant groups.

Around 1500 BC, the ancestors of the present-day **Kalenjin** people entered Kenya from the Nile Valley and displaced the Southern Cushites, although many must have been absorbed in the process, as were some of their customs such as circumcision. These Southern Nilotes were also pastoralists, although there is evidence that sorghum and millet were cultivated. They eventually occupied a large area of central Kenya and because of the region's fertility settled into an agricultural existence. The bulk of Kenya's tea is produced in Kalenjin country.

Another group of Southern Nilotes stayed in the Lake Turkana area and were the ancestors of the present day **Turkana** and **Masai** people. Yet another group, whose descendants, the **Luo**, were to enter Kenya and settle in the Lake Victoria basin about 400 years ago, had moved into what is now western Uganda.

Government Road, now Moi Avenue, Nairobi, around 1906

The vast majority of present-day Kenyans are of **Bantu** origin. Indeed, two-thirds of Africa's entire population is Bantu. They inhabit most of Africa south of the Sahara. The Bantu movement into Kenya was slow and cautious, starting in the first century AD and continuing to the present day. Their first arrival is probably associated with the coming of the Iron Age to sub-Saharan Africa. Although they were both cultivators and cattle herders, the former eventually predominated, causing them to lead a more sedentary life than the other peoples of the region. In consequence their numbers increased and they assumed the majority position they have today.

In the absence of written languages and because what material culture existed has suffered the attrition of time, temperature and termites, very little is definitely known of the activities of the peoples involved in these various immigrations. It is because of this ignorance that historical fable is so rife. Not much credence should be given to the suggestion that the lost tribes of Israel set up house here, nor that King Solomon mined his gold here, nor that the Queen of Sheba's realm encompassed the Great Rift Valley.

The first written record of life and living in Kenya was a seaman's journal, a sort of pilot's guide to the Indian Ocean, called the *Periplus of the Erythraean Sea*. The author, a Greek living in Egypt, wrote this sketchy account around AD 100. Its value lies in its confirmation that a trading community existed before the time of Christ whose connections ranged from the Yemen, the Persian Gulf, and India, as well as the East African coast, and that a money economy existed. Ptolemy, who lived at Alexandria in Egypt in the second century AD, wrote in his great geographical treatise about settlements along the coast of East Africa as well as making more speculative suggestions about the source of the River Nile. This work, together with his map of the world, remained authoritative until the discoveries of the great explorers of the 15th and 16th centuries.

Vasco Da Gama reached Mombasa and Malindi in 1498. His reception in Mombasa was far from welcoming but the Sultan of Malindi, who was having one of his periodic spats with his rival in Mombasa, laid out the red carpet and began a friendly relationship with the Portuguese. This lasted until 1720, when the Arabs and their allies finally drove the remaining Portuguese from the soil of East Africa.

The trading stations that existed, certainly from as early as the second century, gradually spread their roots and an Arab-African culture emerged as the visitors mingled with the local people. This culture, which came to be known as **Swahili**, even today dominates the urban centres of Mombasa, Malindi and Lamu, and its language has become the dominant *lingua franca* of East and Central Africa.

By the ninth century, permanent stone settlements were being built and city-states emerged. Pate, Lamu, Malindi, Gede and Mombasa are the best known of these and their history—of wars between themselves and their would-be invaders—is a fascinating tale of sultans and their slaves, voluptuaries and the religious chaste, and poetry permeating the prosaic.

Da Gama must have returned to Portugal and regaled King John with tales of the inhospitable inhabitants of Mombasa, for two years later a punitive expedition under Cabral attacked and disciplined them. But the major attack was reserved for 1505, when an army of 1,500 men under Francisco D'Almeida challenged the supremacy of Islam and in hand-to-hand fighting pillaged Mombasa. There followed a century and a half of skirmishing between the Muslim Arabs and the Catholic Portuguese, each claiming to be conducting a holy war. The profusion of petty sultanates that stretched along the coast were themselves almost constantly at war with one another, taking sides with Arab or Portuguese as the mood took them. In an attempt to establish lasting authority, the Portuguese built the citadel of Fort Jesus in the last years of the 16th century. This great fortress still dominates the entrance to Mombasa harbour and is now used as a museum.

The East African coast from Somalia to Mozambique is a treasure trove of ruins of the city-states and there are some very fine examples in Kenya. Hauntingly majestic is Gede, near Malindi, a lost city abandoned for no known reason in the 16th century.

The struggle for supremacy between Omani Arabs and the Portuguese continued for another 100 years after the building of Fort Jesus. In 1696, a siege of the fort began that was to last for nearly three years. After the original 3,000 occupants had been reduced by death, desertion and plague to just 13, the Arabs finally scaled the walls, putting the tattered remnants to the sword and extinguishing Portuguese hegemony for ever.

For another century the history of the coast is a sad and miserable record of petty wars between the minor sultanates, and of non- or maladministration by the Omani governors. Trade, other than in humans, subsided until 1822, when Seyyid Said, the Sultan of Oman, sent an army to quell uprisings and rebellions among the coastal population. The heyday of the Arabs was about to dawn.

In 1840, Seyyid Said moved his seat of government from Oman to Zanzibar, where the British, French, Germans and Americans also established a presence. Zanzibar was the entrepôt for East Africa, dealing in slaves, ivory, and agricultural produce. The Kenyan coast had become an important granary, with maize, cassava, cashews and tomatoes being almost the only legacy of 200 years of Portuguese rule. Trade flourished and imports included guns and gunpowder, beads and brass wire, rice, hardware and cotton cloth Much of the last-named came from America and left its own linguistic legacy, since merikani is now a Swahili word meaning cheap cotton material.

The importance of the interior was not only being recognized and exploited by Swahili and Arab caravans but was also being noticed by the European powers, notably Britain and Germany. This interest grew in the second half of the 19th century, one reason being, ostensibly, to eliminate the slave trade. But there were also distinct colonial ambitions, stimulated by exciting stories brought back from the interior by the early explorers such as Burton, Speke and Samuel Baker. The famous 'scramble for Africa' had begun. So unseemly did that scramble become that it was necessary to call a conference to sort out agreed spheres of influence.

In 1885, the Treaty of Berlin gave effective suzerainty of Zanzibar to Britain and most of what is now Kenya and Uganda. Shortly afterwards, Queen Victoria granted a royal charter to the Imperial British East Africa Company, and so began the British occupation of Kenya. In 1895, the British East African Protectorate was declared. This included the whole of mainland Kenya as far as the Great Rift Valley and the island of Zanzibar, from where the territory was administered by the consul-general. It also included, to the east and north, a large area as far as the Juba River, but which in 1925 was ceded to Somaliland. In 1896, work started on construction of a railway line from Mombasa to Uganda. Later to be nicknamed 'the lunatic line', it reached Kisumu on Lake Victoria in 1901. In 1902, the Eastern Province of Uganda was transferred to Kenya, thus ensuring that only one administration was responsible for operation of the railway.

In 1907, the capital was moved from Mombasa to Nairobi and some form of effective British administration took shape. One of the first priorities was to make the railway pay, so immigrant farmer 'settlers' were encouraged. Although most came from Britain, there were also many from South Africa. The settlers included a fair smattering of Britain's aristocracy, partly attracted by the prospect of adventure and the allure of hunting wildlife. Settlement was generally on either side of the railway at altitudes that were comfortable to live at and where the prospects for agriculture could be considered good. This was the area that became known as the 'White High-lands', a permanent and major source of discontent among Africans, who were dispossessed, and a symbol of domination and oppression to all but the settlers themselves.

The first attempt at formal government was made in 1906, when the British created a Legislative Council chaired by the governor; the council was composed of five officials and three nominated white settlers from the few hundred who at that date had colonized the country. This was the first example of the enormous power that the settlers were to wield despite their numerical insignificance—surprising as it may seem, they were never to reach more than 9,000. By 1919, the settlers had achieved elected membership of the Legislative Council, long before any Indian representation was agreed and even longer before a single African sat in such exalted company. It was not until another World War had come and nearly gone before the first African—and then only one—was nominated to the Legislative Council in 1944.

The 1919 Legislative Council, which was the first to contain elected members, signalled the declaration of Kenya as a Colony and Protectorate, the latter being a ten-mile-wide coastal strip stretching from the (then) Tanganyika border to the Sabaki River north of Malindi, which was 'leased' from the Sultan of Zanzibar in 1891. In 1923, the Secretary of State for the Colonies, the Duke of Devonshire, in what was regarded as a sort of Magna Carta for the indigenous people, declared that 'Kenya is an African territory and the interests of the natives must be paramount, and that if and when those interests and the interests of the immigrant races conflict, the former should prevail.'

It was hard, of course, for Kenyan Africans to see that their interests were paramount when they had no representation in either the legislative or the executive processes. For thousands of Africans who had fought alongside the British in the First World War there was no longer any mystique about the white man who, stripped of his technology, was superior only in social and political organization. In 1921, the Young Kikuyu Association was formed, led by Harry Thuku as secretary, who was to have more influence on the future shape of Kenyan politics than he ever could have envisaged. The **Kikuyu** people were in the forefront of Kenyan politics, spurred by their considerable loss of land and by their close physical contact with Nairobi and the seat of government. Thuku saw the dangers of a tribal political organization (apart from its numerical limitations, it offered further opportunity to divide and rule) and soon changed its name to the East African Association.

Kikuyu blacksmiths making a sword, 1931

Missed Connections

She waited for Munira outside the school kei-apple hedge. He got off the metal horse. He stood aside, thinking she only wanted to pass. But she stood in the middle of the narrow track supporting herself against a twigged stick.

'Where you come from: are there tarmac roads?'

'Yes.'

'And light that comes from wires on dry trees to make day out of night?'

'Yes.'

'Women in high heels?'

'Yes.'

'Oiled hair, singed goatskin smell?'

'Yes.'

He looked at her furrowed face, at the light in her eyes. His own wandered past her, over the empty school, for it was after four o'clock, and he thought: what did she want?

'They are beautiful and wise in the ways of the white man: is this not so?'

'That they are: too wise, sometimes.'

'Our young men and women have left us. The glittering metal has called them. They go, and the young women only return now and then to deposit the newborn with their grandmothers already aged with scratching this earth for a morsel of life. They say: there in the city there is room for only one. . . our employers, they don't want babies about the tiny rooms in tiny yards. Have you ever heard of that? Unwanted children? The young men also. Some go and never return. Others sometimes come to see the wives *they left behind, make them round-bellied, and quickly go away as if driven from Ilmorog by Uhere (measles) or Mutung'u (smallpox). What should we call them? The new Uhere and Mutung'u generation: for was it not the same skin diseases and plagues that once in earlier times weakened our people in face of the Mzungu invasion? Tell me: what then brings you to a deserted homestead? Look at Abdulla. He came from over there and what did he bring us? A donkey. Now imagine, a donkey! What have you really come to fetch from our village? Is it the remaining children?'*

He pondered this a few seconds. He plucked a ripened yellow kei-apple and crushed it between his fingers: isn't there a safe corner in which to hide and do some work, plant a seed whose fruits one could see? *The smell from the rotting fermenting kei-apple hit into his nostrils. He felt a sudden nausea,* Lord deliver us from our past, *and frantically fumbled in his pockets for a handkerchief to cover the sneeze. It was too late. A bit of mucus flew onto the woman's furrowed face. She shrieked out,* auuu-u, Nduri ici mutiuke muone, *and fled in fright. He turned his face aside to hold back another sneeze. When a second later he looked to the path, he could not find a trace of her behind the kei-apple bush or anywhere. She had vanished.*

Strange, mysterious, he muttered to himself. He got on his metal horse and slowly rode toward Abdulla's shop.

Ngugi wa Thiong'o, Petals of Blood

There was plenty to campaign about. The land question was always there, as was the detested pass system and the hut tax, and it was not long before demonstrations turned into riots. On 15 March 1922, the authorities arrested Thuku and detained him overnight in the Central Police Station. The next day a great crowd assembled outside the station—where the University of Nairobi now stands—taunting the police to release Thuku. The police responded with rifles and 21 people were shot dead. Thuku was detained and deported to Kismaiyu, where he stayed until his release in 1931. The East African Association was banned but it was not long before its successor appeared on the scene, this time to be led by someone who, much later, was to become affectionately known as 'the father of the nation', Jomo Kenyatta.

The dominant African voice in the period between the two world wars was to be that of the Kikuyu Central Association. Formed in 1924, originally with the release of Thuku as its main purpose, it quickly grew in membership and ambitions, especially after Kenyatta became its secretary-general in 1928. Land was its principal concern, although education and political representation were also prominent objectives. It was a time of great economic hardship. Even before the collapse of the New York Stock Exchange in 1929, Kenya had been devastated by a series of locust invasions and a famine relief board was operating. It was partly as a result of the failure of the settler-dominated economy that Lord Moyne was sent out to Kenya by the Colonial Office to head a delegation charged with assessing the need for economic reforms.

Moyne pinpointed the vulnerability of an economy hitherto reliant on the price-sensitive crops produced by the settler farmers, when the colony's principal source of income was tax paid by an African population whose capacity in the agricultural field had been unrecognized. A direct consequence of the Moyne delegation was a rapid expansion of African agriculture, culminating in the lifting of the ban on African coffee-growing in 1937.

Greater effort was also made in education. Many of the educational facilities that existed at the time were created by missionaries and faced problems arising from a conflict between traditional African culture and imported church law. For example, in 1929 the Church of Scotland mission expelled those of its members who ignored a church ruling forbidding female circumcision. The rest of the Protestant community followed suit, providing the Kikuyu Central Association with an unexpected political weapon.

The influence of the KCA was greatly expanded and led directly to the formation of the Kikuyu Independent Schools Association, a movement that had a much wider influence on the future of Kenya than has hitherto been recognized. In 1929, Kenyatta left for England, alone, in an attempt to see the colonial secretary, despite a warning by the government in Nairobi that he would not be seen. He never did manage to meet the colonial secretary, although he did see the under-secretary, who was alarmed at a visit Kenyatta had made to Russia but in the end reported favourably on him to the governor.

Kenyatta returned to Kenya in 1930, in time to see Harry Thuku released from eight years in detention. A behind-the-scenes leadership struggle left Kenyatta the loser. However, more money was collected to send him back to London in 1931 in an unofficial attempt to appear before a joint select committee of Parliament that had been appointed to look into the problems of the three East African territories. He failed in this regard but yet another commission was set up to look into the land rights of Kenyan Africans. Kenyatta, still in London, appeared before the Carter Commission, as it was known, in June 1932. It was to be another 14 years before he returned to Kenya.

Nearly 100,000 Kenyan Africans saw service with the British during the Second World War. Their discipline and their bravery contributed to the defeat of the Italian army in Ethiopia, the Vichy French in Madagascar, and the Japanese in Burma. Not only did these victories engender a new, wider concept of nationalism but the exposure to other colonized peoples in Palestine, India, Ceylon, and Aden laid the foundations of a truly national outlook that was to emerge after the war.

The appointment of Eliud Mathu as the first African member of the Legislative Council in 1944 was accompanied by the formation of a body known as the Kenya African Study Union. The idea was that this union would be the contact point between Mathu and the people, who themselves were represented by some 15 prominent persons nominated to the union's committee and led by Harry Thuku. The word 'Study' was soon dropped, as was Harry Thuku, now considered too sympathetic to the settler viewpoint.

The Kenya African Union, led by James Gichuru, became the voice of African nationalism. Jomo Kenyatta returned to Kenya in January 1946 to a hero's welcome, and it was not long before he took over the leadership of the party. The years before the declaration of a state of emergency in October 1952 saw an inevitable clash between radicals and reactionaries within the party, with Kenyatta playing a mediating role. The radicals, by definition noisier and more obvious than the others, were assisted by the large number of unemployed ex-servicemen who had migrated to the towns. Despite a great effort by the colonial government, the demobilization and resettlement of ex-servicemen was scarcely a success story and open bitterness and resentment was rife. Those who were planning armed rebellion found plenty of willing recruits.

On 20 October 1952, the governor, Sir Evelyn Baring, declared a state of emergency and Mau Mau, a secret society about which practically nothing was known, was proscribed. On the same evening the security forces mounted an operation codenamed 'Jock Scott', detaining large numbers of people, among them the leaders of

KAU and including its president, Jomo Kenyatta. The emergency lasted four years, and although the Mau Mau movement had sympathizers among other tribes, it was almost entirely confined to the Kikuyu and their relatives, the **Embu** and **Meru**.

The uprising had little cohesion and less strategy; its ideals seemed most attractive to the young and uneducated. The consequence was a division of the tribes into Mau Mau adherents and 'loyalists', the latter composed of civil servants, Christians, the better educated and the better off. The hatred engendered between these two groups is apparent more than 30 years since the end of hostilities. There are no reliable figures of casualties but it is estimated that at least 10,000 Africans died on both sides. Less than 50 Europeans perished in the fighting. With the capture of Dedan Kimathi in 1956 the shooting war was over, leaving nearly 30,000 people in detention whose re-absorption into post-emergency society was to take another three years. For a few, it took even longer. Jomo Kenyatta himself was not finally released until the second half of 1961.

With the ending of the emergency there was a flurry of activity at the Colonial Office, matched by an unprecedented growth in African nationalism. In 1957, the first direct elections of Africans to the Legislative Assembly were held. It was not so much the advent of eight elected African members that was important as the legitimacy of those members. After all, they were not the first Africans to sit in government, but they were the first who were not appointed by the colonial authorities. Thus, the voices advocating independence not only rang out more stridently but they did so from within the system. One of those first eight elected members was Daniel arap Moi, who was to succeed to the presidency upon the death of Kenyatta in 1978.

An early triumph was the convening of a constitutional conference in London in January 1960. The Lancaster House Conference was a total victory for the African cause, producing a constitution that gave a majority to the Africans in the Legislature and a four-to-three ratio in the Council of Ministers. It should be remembered that British prime minister, Harold MacMillan, made his famous 'Wind of Change' speech whilst the Lancaster House Conference was in progress.

By now, two major political parties had been formed by Africans—the Kenya African National Union (KANU) and the Kenya African Democratic Union (KADU). In the 1961 election, KANU held 19 seats to KADU's 11 but refused to form a government until Kenyatta was released. The governor was forced to ask KADU to form a minority government, which it did by joining forces with the European and Asian elected members of the Legislative Council. But keeping Kenyatta in restriction was too difficult a task in the heady air of 1961, and in that year the governor, Sir Patrick Renison, finally released the man whom he had called a 'leader unto darkness and death'. A few months later, a KANU member of the legislature resigned his seat and Kenyatta entered the Legislative Council unopposed. In April 1962, KANU and

KADU formed a reluctant coalition government in which Kenyatta became Minister of State for Constitutional Affairs and Economic Planning and KADU's leader, Ronald Ngala, the Minister of State for Constitutional Affairs and Administration.

The last pre-independence election was held in May 1963 and proved a decisive victory for KANU. Jomo Kenyatta became prime minister on 1 June 1963 and less than six months later, on 12 December, Kenya became totally independent. It did so with a curious brand of regional government introduced into the constitution to appease KADU, a head of state (the British monarch represented by a governor-general), and a head of government, the prime minister. Within a year KADU virtually ceased to exist, all it members crossing the floor to join KANU.

On the first anniversary of its independence, Kenya became a republic with Kenyatta its first president. He faced a daunting array of difficulties in almost every direction. There were still many racial imbalances, tribal problems were magnified by political allegiances, land hunger was serious, the call for improved social services was strident, and economic growth and development projects stifled by the lack of capital and trained manpower. Within the party there was a faction that saw communism—or at least socialism—as the panacea. In an effort to contain the radicals, Kenyatta's faction produced a somewhat hazy policy document entitled *African Socialism and its Application to Planning in Kenya*. For the less informed, 'African Socialism' became a sort of political cult; for others, it was patently window-dressing.

In 1966, a group of members of parliament led by the vice-president split from KANU and formed the Kenya People's Party (KPU). The 30 MPs who formed the new party were almost all **Luo** from western Kenya, and although there was a smattering of other tribal groups, it was impossible to describe the new party as a national one. Its role in parliament as the official opposition was short-lived. Within 24 hours, KANU introduced a constitutional amendment; it required those members of parliament who had defected from the party to which they were elected to resign and seek a fresh mandate. In the election that followed, 29 seats were contested, and only seven KPU members were returned to the Lower House and two to the Senate.

KPU was tolerated, uneasily, for three years but in 1969 was banned after a visit by the president to Kisumu in western Kenya, when he came very close to being involved in serious rioting. So Kenya became, once again, a de facto one-party state. In July 1966, Tom Mboya—perhaps the most articulate of the pre- and post-independence politicians—was assassinated, probably because his murderers saw him as a threat to the Kenyatta succession.

That succession was not to be for another 12 years, a period marked by economic growth and an increasing polarization of the rich and the poor—and by the dominance of the Kikuyu, whose hold on the civil service was matched only by the number of its economic giants. One politician, J M Kariuki, by now the most eloquent opponent of a system he saw becoming more corrupt, more neglectful of the mass of the population, and more heedless of the plight of the unemployed, was silenced. In March 1974, Kariuki disappeared after a social meeting at the Nairobi Hilton hotel and was later found murdered in deserted territory not far from the capital.

Kenyatta died in his sleep in August 1978, and to the surprise of many, the succession was constitutional. The new president, Daniel arap Moi, was welcomed as a sincere opponent of tribalism and corruption, the two most marked stigma of the first 15 years of independence. He introduced his own philosophy of Peace, Love and Unity to a country sadly in need of all of these qualities, and took a much more aggressive interest in international affairs.

The first few years of the new presidency saw a wave of student protests. Despite the tolerance that allowed them to take place at all, these protests ended almost annually with the closing of the university, and with student misbehaviour occupying the attention of the public, various members of the university's academic staff cultivated more radical political designs. In 1982, there was a series of detentions of left-wing politicians and university staff, but the worst was to come on 1 August, a Sunday, when Kenya's hitherto peaceful record of political and economic growth was shattered by an attempted *coup d'état* staged by junior members of the Air Force. Within three days the coup had been suppressed, but not before there were hundreds of deaths in the streets of Nairobi, and looting, rape and pillage had brought the capital to the brink of mob rule.

Since 1982 there has been steady, if not dramatic, progress in the economy, with coffee and tea the most important contributors from the agricultural sector, and tourism now the single largest foreign exchange earner. On the political front, KANU's influence in politics grew ever stronger to the point where it was difficult to tell whether parliament or the party was supreme. However, far from silencing opposing voices, KANU's strength has engendered ever more determination in the opposition. Aided by Western political and financial pressures, the latter forced President Moi to concede the repeal of the clause in the constitution that limited Kenya to a one-party system. In December 1991, the constitution was amended by the same government that introduced the limiting clause in 1982, with the result that a legal multi-party democracy came into being. The first elections under this new system must be held by 1993.

Chief Kinyanjui Wa Gatharimu, a friend of Karen Blixen, 1910

Kenya's People

Archeological evidence suggests that northern Kenya was indeed the 'Cradle of Man-kind'. In the harsh deserts on the eastern shore of Lake Turkana, remains of fossil hominids—early man—have been uncovered, dating more than three million years. Although present-day Kenya, with nearly 25 million people, is one nation of consid-erable and growing cohesion, it is built on the shoulders of diverse groups of people, each contributing to its heritage and its culture. This kaleidoscope of cultures is very much a part of the country's fascination, and something that is of constant interest to visitors. But as part of the nation-building process, Kenyans have been urged to subli-mate their tribal allegiances for the national good, and to some extent this exhortation has succeeded. Kenyans are proud of being Kenyans—but they are also proud of their ethnic origins.

Oral, archeological and linguistic evidence indicates that Kenya has been the centre of three major migrations—the **Cushites** from the north and northeast some 9,000 years ago, the **Bantu** from the western forests around AD 1000, and more re-cently, at the end of the 16th century, the **Nilotes** from the Nile area of what is now Sudan. Only three small groups of the ancestral inhabitants remain in modern Kenya: the **Ndorobo**, the **Boni** and the **Sanye**.

The Bantu are agriculturalists and live in the fertile highland area of central Ken-ya, along the coast, and in two large communities in western Kenya. In addition to those communities, the western third of Kenya is the home of the Nilotic people, some of whom are agriculturalists, some pastoralists, and some nomads. The Cushitic group occupies a huge area of north and northeastern Kenya, an arid, semi-desert region, and in consequence most of the inhabitants are nomads.

Within the Bantu group, and indeed within the whole of Kenya, the **Kikuyu**, or sometimes **Gikuyu**, and their close neighbours the **Embu** and the **Meru** are the most numerous, totalling around 6.5 million. The next largest group among the Bantu are the **Luhya**, who occupy the three districts of Bungoma, Busia, and Kakamega, which together form the Western Province. The Luhya are estimated to number about 3 million. Then, still in numerical order, are the **Kamba** (**Akamba**) (about 2.5 million), famed the world over for their wood carving; the **Kisii** (**Gusii**) from the highlands east of Lake Victoria (1.5 million); and the **Mijikenda** from the coast littoral (1.3 million).

The Nilotic people are represented by the **Luo**, whose distant origins are in what is now the Sudan. Currently numbering about 2.8 million, they occupy three districts abutting Lake Victoria. The Luo are diligent farmers in circumstances that are not easy. In Luo-land rain tends to fall in either over- or under-abundance, so flood and famine have contributed to their stoic attitudes.

A Topasa woman wearing coiled torques of wire—a wedding gift from her husband

Luo traditional dress is the most decorative in Kenya. Body ornamentation, to-gether with colourful headgear of ostrich feathers, hippo tusks and metal jewellry, make Luo dances and festivities an eye-catching scene. Music is important to the Luo. Haunting melodies are produced from a one-stringed lyre called *orutu* played with a sisal bow and from the eight-stringed *thum* lyre. They have a wide range of cultural skills, including boat building of course, but also basketry and pottery. The latter extends to a fearsome array of clay pipes for smoking locally grown tobacco.

The Cushitic group is itself divided into two, the Southern and Eastern, the latter now represented by the **Somali** and the **Rendille**. The Southern group are no longer represented in Kenya, having either been absorbed by the Nilotes who followed them several hundred years later, or having passed through the country and settled mainly in today's Tanzania. In the process of this absorption they left behind a considerable number of their customs and some of their language to be adopted by the Southern Nilotes. Among these people are the **Kalenjin**, a group living in the Rift Valley Province of Kenya and comprising (in order of numerical importance) the **Kipsigis**, the **Nandi**, the **Tugen**, the **Pokot**, the **Elgeyo**, and the **Marakwet**. All these people are highland agriculturalists, although it should be noted that in today's Kenya millions of people have left their agricultural, nomadic, or pastoralist origins and settled in towns or other areas of the country. An interesting cultural feature of the Kalenjin is a learning programme of ancient customs and traditional values, which is set up for both sexes after initiation. A phenomenon not entirely understood is that very many of Kenya's world-famous long-distance runners are Kalenjin.

The **Masai**, part of the Eastern Nilotic group, and so named because they speak Maa, are relatively small in numbers (less than 650,000) but for all that are probably Kenya's best known tribe. In earlier times they provided a formidable military force quite out of proportion to their numbers. 'I hope your cattle flourish' is a typical Masai greeting, and one that symbolizes the deep involvement that these people have with their cattle. Cattle not only represent wealth, but supply food (meat, milk and blood), provide leather for beds, sandals, and also provide a currency for marriage, fines and sacrifices.

Life for a Masai is indeed a series of ceremonies and celebrations. These lead through initiation to junior warriorhood, then to senior warriorhood, before junior and senior elder. Respect from everyone is due to the *Ol Laiboni*, a mixture of proph-ets and priests, the most famous of whom are from one family and whose names are perpetuated in the peaks of Mount Kenya: Nelion, Batian, and Lenana.

The **Samburu** are relatives of the Masai and number around 100,000. They occu-py a huge district of about 26,000 square kilometres (10,000 square miles), stretch-ing from the Uaso Ngwiro River in the south, to Lake Turkana in the north. At one time the Masai, the Samburu, and another related group, the **Njemps**, used to live

THE SAMBURU

Samburu District, in which most of the Samburu people live, is not the biggest district in Kenya, but is nevertheless very large. Its 26,000 square kilometres (10,000 square miles) are mostly arid and often mountainous and it is definitely country in which only the hardy can survive. The Samburu are not numerous— less than 90,000 souls—and the majority live in the central plateau, called *Lorroki* (often anglicized to Leroghi on maps), where the rainfall is twice the district average.

Legend has it that the Loikop (Samburu) originated in a place called Oto, thought to be in present-day Ethiopia. On their southward migration they sheltered in the mountain country of Marsabit and Mount Nyiro, and the hostility of the now defunct Laikipia tribe kept them there. The Laikipia were overcome by the joint action of the Maa-speaking tribes in about 1870, and the area became the territory of the Samburu. The five Maa-speaking tribes—Masai, Lchamus (Njemps), Ltorrobo (Nderobo), Lmokokodo (Mukogodo) and the Loikop—all used to live adjacent to one another until white settlement broke up this contiguity. The word Samburu (or more correctly *Sampurr*) was merely the Masai nickname for the Loikop, who carried their prized possessions in a bag on their backs called a *sampurr*. Another version—that the name arises from the word meaning 'butterfly' (this is actually *sampirr-pirr*)—is more apocryphal. In reality, the five Maa-speakers are all clans of one huge tribe. These clans are basically the same people having similar customs and a common language. The Samburu and the Lchamus share one accent and speak faster than the other three clans. The Masai and the Lmokogodo also share an accent and both speak relatively slowly. Besides speech, the differences between, say, Masai and Samburu are hard to find. One example, however, is that of personal decoration and adornment. The Samburu pay much more attention to detail than the Masai, and the result is decoration that is finer, neater and also more lavish.

Samburu girl

The Samburu live communally in small groups of settlements called *manyat*. A *manyatta* (the singular of *manyat*) may be of one family or several, but in the latter case is usually of one sub-clan. Given the nomadic nature of the people, these *manyat* are extremely temporary. As long as pasture and water last, the *manyatta* stays put. A Samburu settlement is composed of a number of loaf-shaped huts arranged in a circular form and surrounded by a thorn barrier. The first wife's hut is to the right of the main (cattle) entrance. This arrangement holds even when there is more than one family in a settlement. The elders decide according to custom which family should take what position in the circle. If a *manyatta* remains in the same locale despite the shortage of water and grazing, the young people move with the livestock to areas of fresh pasture. Here they build simple settlements called *laletta*. These do not require the formalities of a *manyatta* and quite often not even huts are built. A small thorn enclosure is partitioned into a place for a fire and for sleeping. Unless wildlife becomes a threat to life and livestock, the Samburu live peaceably with game. When a lion, for instance, becomes a menace to livestock, it is hunted and killed by the *moran*, men of the warrior grade. The Samburu hunted wildlife in times of severe food shortage but were extremely selective, killing only hoofed animals: elephant and rhino were never part of the food supply. No doubt this was a major reason for the abundance of these two species in the district prior to the formulation of Kenya's game laws.

next to one another, but they were divided at the turn of the century by European settlement. Two differences between the Samburu and the Masai are immediately apparent even to a stranger. Firstly, the Samburu speak much faster than their relatives and, secondly, their body decoration is more lavish.

The **Turkana** belong to the Eastern Nilotic group and inhabit an inhospitable area of great size, 67,000 square kilometres (26,800 square miles), to the west of Lake Turkana. They are principally a pastoral people but they also hunt, gather honey, and sometimes fish. Their marginal environment has perfected their survival techniques and the Turkana are fearless fighters. The basic social unit is the family and their simple homesteads reflect the ever-present need for mobility. The camel is the main source of life and wealth for the Turkana. Men herd the camels, which are milked by women. Perhaps surprisingly, the Turkana have a highly developed aesthetic taste, displayed in remarkable personal adornment and a wide craft field. In the first category are the hairstyles of the men, often so elaborate that they require the use of a neck stool for sleeping. Their crafts utilize the natural materials of the area—leather, wood, seeds, shells, horns, bones, stones, tusks and feathers are all employed.

Zebras at a waterhole, Tsavo West National Park

Nairobi

On 30 May 1899, the 'lunatic line', the railway from Mombasa, reached Nairobi. Colonel Patterson, author of *The Man-eaters of Tsavo,* wrote: 'There was an immense amount of work to be done in converting an absolutely bare plain, 327 miles from the nearest place where even a nail could be purchased, into a busy railway centre.' Such problems seemed not to daunt either the railway workers or their attendant civilian following, for 'Wonderfully soon, however, the nucleus of the present town began to take shape, and a thriving bazaar sprang into existence with a mushroom-like growth.'

None of the railway staff envisaged that a capital city would emerge; they sought only to establish the headquarters of the railway and to draw breath before tackling the hilly country ahead. In 1898, the Uganda Railway Committee (of the British Parliament) commissioned Sir Guildford Molesworth to inspect the line. In his report he wrote, 'Nyrobi has, with great judgement, been selected as the site for the principal workshops. It is about 5,500 feet above the level of the sea, which ensures a comparatively salubrious climate: there is ample space of level ground for all requirements, and excellent sites for the quarters of officers and subordinates, on higher ground above the station site. There is a fairly good supply of water, but reservoirs and tanks will have to be constructed.'

The Masai name N*yrobi* (or *Nyarobe*) indicates that it is a place of cold water, having reference of course to the *Ngare Nyrobi*, the Nairobi River and its attendant swamps.The commercial growth of the town was centred on the river, then used for drinking but now so polluted that only the extremely hardy, or rather foolhardy, would consider this use of its water.The word 'river' connotes a wholly inaccurate picture, for the Nairobi River is little more than a stream and certainly not worth a visit!

Within a year of the beginning of the construction of railway yards, the bazaar had taken real shape in the area now occupied by Moi Avenue. Plague broke out and the worthy Colonel Patterson dealt with that problem by incinerating the newly-built huts and hovels. But that was merely a temporary interruption to Nairobi's growth. Within three years of the railway's arrival, cars appeared on the streets (a rather grand word for what were in truth mud tracks) and Nairobi had earned a mention on the map. Some semblance of order began with the appointment of a municipal committee in 1901, and its future was sealed with the move of the capital from Mombasa to Nairobi in 1906. Growth has never been orderly, since both the growth rate and migration into the town have always totally outpaced the ability of the authorities to provide infrastructure and social requirements. During the Second World War the population rose by an incredible 15 per cent per year, and even today Nairobi doubles its numbers every seven years. The majority of the migrants arrive penniless, in search of work, and merely add to the multitudes living in the slums and 'cardboard cities'. In 1991, Nairobi had an estimated population of about 1.6 million.

Accommodation

The average foreign visitor to the capital observes only the vibrant, cosmopolitan city centre where its international-class hotels are situated, and perhaps some of the sub-urbs where Nairobi's more affluent inhabitants live. Two of the world's great hotel chains, **Inter-Continental** and **Hilton** have had hotels in the city centre for 20 years and will shortly be joined by **Meridien**, which (in mid-1991) is at the planning and construction stage. The independently owned and managed all-suite **Nairobi Safari Club** rivals, in terms of comfort and amenities, the world-famous **Norfolk Hotel** not far away. The **Nairobi Serena**, the **Panafric**, the **Sixeighty** and the **New Stanley** are all of international class and are either in or close to the city centre.

Eight kilometres (five miles) from the city centre is the **Utalii Hotel**. This is the government's application hotel for Kenya Utalii College, which has earned an international reputation as Africa's leading hotel and tourism training centre. Another three kilometres (one and a half miles) along the Thika road is the latest international class hotel, the **Safari Park**, a luxurious interpretation of African style set in a huge and imaginatively landscaped garden. Recently opened, ten kilometres (six miles) from downtown Nairobi is the new **Windsor Golf and Country Club**, a sumptuous establishment sporting a fine 18-hole golf course.

Visitors who are more price conscious could consider the **Ambassadeur**, very near the Hilton in the city centre, or the **Boulevard** a little way beyond the Norfolk. Five kilometres (three miles) farther out in the same direction is the **Jacaranda**. Utalii, Safari Park, Windsor Golf and the Jacaranda all operate courtesy bus services to the city centre at frequent intervals.

Shopping

The main tourist shopping areas are contained within a rough rectangle, no more than a kilometre on its longest side and limited in the west by Uhuru Highway, in the north by University Way, thence in a southerly direction by Moi Avenue, and completing the rectangle by City Hall Way.

Nairobi City Centre

Legend: ★ Hotel

| 0 | 100 | 200 | 300 m |
| 0 | 100 | 200 | 300 yards |

Ngara Road

Nairobi River

Kirinyaga Road

Keekorok Road

River Road

Meridian Court

Moi Avenue

Kumasi Road

Mosque

Latema Road

River Road

Tom

Mboya

River Road

Racecourse Road

cMillan Library

Kimathi Street

New Stanley ★

Street

Street

Luthuli Avenue

Ngala Street

Standard Street

Wabera Street

Ngina Street

National Archives

★ Ambassadeur

Nairobi ★ Hilton

Ronald Ngala Street

Mama Ngina St

Hall Way

Moi Avenue

Tom Mboya Street

Bus ■ Terminal

City

Aga Khan Walk

Taifa Road

Avenue

Square

Kenyatta Conference Centre

Harambee Avenue

Selassie

Haile

■ Post Office

Workshops Road

Nairobi Railway Station ■

Railway Museum

6th Avenue, Nairobi in 1929, later Delamere Avenue, now Kenyatta Avenue.
The building called 'The Motor Mart' is now the location of the 680 Hotel

Handicrafts are the best buys: woodcarving, soapstone carving, beadwork, batiks and baskets are the most common and, not surprisingly, vary from the sophisticated and artistic to the cheap and nasty. Perhaps a good place to start looking is in the craft market near the city market, just behind the splendid **Jamia Mosque**. Wander safely through this labyrinth of kiosks before deciding what to buy, and certainly don't buy anything at the asking price. In the markets and in the streets just give the impression that you are an expert on the right price structure of Kenyan crafts. Decide how much the item is worth and haggle until you get that price or until the vendor makes it clear he is not selling.

Having made a survey of the market, now look at some of the more sophisticated shops. Here, you do not haggle but you request a discount! You may find that the discounted price for a better finished article is not all that different from the street price. **African Heritage**, in Kenyatta Avenue, is one of the best known of the craft emporia and is unique in having a fixed price policy. Its prices are generally high but so is the quality. Good craft shops are scattered throughout the city centre and there are far too many good ones to mention all by name. In shopping for crafts you should also remember that you will find plenty on safari and getting closer to the producer, as it were, may result in a better bargain. But with carvings, you are unlikely to find the beautiful finishes that can be found in Nairobi galleries.

In the city market, which looks like an aircraft hangar, is a mass of fruit and vegetable stalls, overlooked from an encircling gallery by a profusion of small curio shops. If you exit through the back door of the city market you will find an area entirely devoted to baskets and basketwork.

Gemstones can be good buys, although that may not turn out to be the case if you try to bargain on the streets. Fine specimens of jasper, blue-lace agate, fluorspar, malachite, sodalite, petrified wood, and many, many others can be found without difficulty. Two stones stand out for their rarity and their value: tanzanite, a brilliant blue but distinguished from sapphire by its purple tinge; and tsavorite, which is not unlike emerald. Unmounted, these stones can be bought in Nairobi for half their New York price. Other interesting local stones are malaya garnets, rubies, and amethysts. Rock hounds, too, will find plenty to interest and excite them.

The best of many of Kenya's products and crafts can be found under one roof in **Utamaduni** in the suburb of Langata. You can call in there on the way to the Giraffe Centre or the Karen Blixen Museum.

Shopping in Kenya is not complete without mention of the *kiondo*. This is a hand-woven sisal string basket that can be slung over the shoulder or carried as a shopping bag. Usually cheerfully coloured, it is nowadays often trimmed with leather. So successful has it been as a utility object and a fashion accessory that it has been copied by other developing countries and exported to Kenya's traditional overseas markets.

The sale of game trophies or objects made from them is illegal. So the 'elephant hair' bracelets that you will be offered on the streets are either illegal or made of plastic, more likely the latter. The 'lion claws', mounted in gold and found in quite sophisticated shops, are made from camels' hooves.

Sights

Exploration begins with the **National Museum**, one and a half kilometres (one mile) from the city centre. The museum's strengths are in its ethnological and pre-history sections, the latter displaying many of the finds of the late Dr Louis Leakey and his son Richard, now the Director of the Kenya Wildlife Service. Joy Adamson, of *Born Free* fame, was an accomplished artist and the originals of her portraits of the peoples of Kenya and her superb paintings of indigenous flowers of Kenya are also on display. The collections of mammals, birds and butterflies are extensive, as befits a country so richly endowed by nature, and these galleries provide a wonderful check on all your unidentified safari finds. There is a small shop in the museum. The museum is open every day of the year from 9 am to 6 pm.

Nearby is a **snake park** and an **aquarium**, the former very much visited by those visitors anxious to see some of Kenya's more than 100 species of venomous snakes.

Quite close to the railway station is the **Railway Museum**, a gem for anyone interested in Kenya's history over the last century and, again for the morbidly curious, housing the actual carriage from which Superintendent Ryall was dragged and eaten by a 'man-eater of Tsavo' in 1897. At one time the railway was under the same administration as the harbours, so the museum also displays some maritime exhibits, among them relics of the German battleship *Königsberg*, which sunk in the delta of a Tanzanian river in 1917. In the museum yard are a number of steam engines, obviously a draw for those who mourn the passing of that era. The Railway Museum is open from 9 am to 4 pm, Mondays through Fridays.

The **Karen Blixen Museum**, some 20 kilometres (12 miles) from the city centre, is found in the suburb that bears her name. The rooms contain more nostalgia than memorabilia, and when found, the latter could be flotsam from the set of *Out of Africa* rather than the real thing. But the building that houses the museum was indeed Blixen's, and apart from its intrinsic charm, a visit is justified for its revelations of colonial Kenya.

Daisy Rothschild's relatives and friends live on at **Giraffe Manor**, not far from the Blixen Museum. Near the manor is the Giraffe Centre (or more properly the **Langata Nature Education Centre**) where you can not only find out all there is to know about giraffes, but can actually feed these gentle creatures as they come in from the surrounding countryside every afternoon at 4 pm to see their visitors. This is the chance to observe the remarkable tongue (45 centimetres, about 18 inches, long and covered with a very tough skin; its tip, with which it seizes food, bears many small fleshy spines).

An exciting and elegant (though expensive) experience is to stay at Giraffe Manor. Now being tastefully enlarged, it nevertheless remains a quiet and decorous reminder of a bygone age. Where else would you find a giraffe joining you for afternoon tea? There is a delightful nature walk (of about one kilometre, half a mile) through the estate, where you might chance upon a bushbuck but will definitely see plenty of the 180 odd species of birds found there.

'**Bomas of Kenya**', near the entrance to Nairobi National Park, is a government-sponsored exhibition of traditional music and dance as well as a demonstration of indigenous building styles and handicrafts. Over-long and sadly presented, the dance repertoire is nevertheless worth a visit if only for the highlights—the Samburu, Wakamba and Mjikenda dancers.

A rather different kind of sightseeing tour takes place every Wednesday at 8.30 am. This is the **Bird-Watchers Walk**, starting at the National Museum and lasting a couple of hours. No charge is made, and it is an excellent opportunity to meet a few

The Karen Blixen Museum, near Nairobi

Supply and Demand

If the hunters only rarely came out of the bush, the same could be said of the farmers, who trekked into Nairobi maybe two or three times a year to buy stores, sell their produce, get their machinery repaired and trade gossip with anyone else who happened to be in town. Serious men normally, they always advanced on the capital with a purposeful glint in their eye, determined to cram six months' riotous living into a stay of a week or so, knowing that the opportunity would not come again for some considerable time. Nairobi offered the chance to hear the swish of a woman's skirt, read a newspaper, have a drink with friends, and then investigate that skirt. The laws of supply and demand being what they are, a white woman in Kenya had to be very ugly indeed not to wrest a halting proposal from some hat-holding settler who had been practising his speech for weeks on his best Hereford and had now forgotten every word of it. And for those not interested in marriage, a new Japanese whore house had been established where you could take your chance with a slanteyed Oriental bint and chuck the furniture into the street if you were not satisfied.

Of course, not all Europeans had a craving for feminine company. Some people came to Kenya specifically to get away from women. A man who thought himself secure at the far end of Nandi country was dismayed to receive an irate message from his superior at Nandi fort: 'A woman in men's clothes who says she is your wife has emerged from behind my office safe. Come here at once and identify her or deny the allegation by helio message.'

Nicholas Best, Happy Valley:
The Story of the English in Kenya

like-minded Kenyans or residents. Bird-watchers may also take a ride out to the suburb of Langata where **Pat Frere** shows visitors around his bird-infested garden. Go in time for afternoon tea, shared by the birds, which offers a chance to see the African black kite's superb aerobatics. Another place to watch birds, and also enjoy solitude and peace, is the **Nairobi Arboretum**, a short taxi ride from the city centre, where there are 32 hectares (80 acres) of lawns and carefully labelled trees.

The main visitor attraction at Nairobi is, of course, the **Nairobi National Park**, eight kilometres (five miles) from the city on the way to the suburbs of Karen and Langata, and therefore possible to combine with a visit to 'Bomas' or the Karen Blixen Museum. There are times when the park is seemingly full of wildlife: in September, for example, herds of wildebeest invade the park as grazing becomes short in the surrounding plains. But there are also times when wildlife is less abundant, although it is almost impossible not to see giraffe, several species of antelope, baboon and nowadays rhino, as so many have been translocated to the park for safety.

At the beginning of a safari, or on a day off for the executive on a business visit, the Nairobi National Park is never a disappointment. Almost all the mammals found in other Kenyan parks are found here with the exception of the elephant, and the birds are prolific. At the southeastern end of the park you can walk in a beautiful acacia forest and search for hippo and crocodile in the nearby river. This is the place to have a picnic, but be warned of the fearless vervet monkeys that will try and share it with you. Lion, leopard and cheetah can all be found (but rarely at the picnic site!) and searching for these predators will not only keep your hunting instincts honed but increase the appreciation of your eagle-eyed Kenyan driver-guide, who seems so effortlessly able to spot the invisible. At the main entrance to the park is the **Animal Orphanage**, which is best avoided unless a makeshift zoo appeals to you. The park opens at 6.15 am and closes at 6.30 pm every day of the year.

The **National Archives**, in Moi Avenue just across from the Hilton, also house an art gallery and a collection of ethnographical material. Both of these suffer from poor or non-existent labelling but are still worth a visit. The archives themselves are not open to visitors without a research permit, but anyone interested in looking into Kenya's written history can use the extensive reference material in the **McMillan Library** in Banda Street.

Gallery Watatu, in Standard Street, is the leading private art gallery, where there is always a representative collection (for sale) of original works by African artists. A smaller gallery that often has some good original wildlife paintings is the **Monaco** in City Hall Way. Robin Anderson's exquisite batiks on silk are found only in her gallery, **Tazama**, in Standard Street very near to Gallery Watatu. Exhibitions by local artists are held very often at the German, French and British cultural centres. The daily newspapers carry details of these.

There are plenty of interesting places to visit within an easy day's drive from Nairobi. None of these are currently on tour operators' scheduled trips, but all can be arranged at short notice or you can hire a car and drive yourself. **Lake Naivasha**, 84 kilometres (52 miles) from the city centre, is reached by a fast, modern road and is a particularly easy and extremely scenic drive. From this road there are breathtaking views of the **Great Rift Valley** studded with extinct volcanoes, among them the almost perfect cone of **Mount Longonot**, which can be climbed without mountaineering skills but which requires a degree of fitness.

If you are fit, head for the railway station described as 'Longonot' on the map, where there are a few shops and a police post. This is the place to leave your car and find a suitable guide. It will take you about two hours to reach the crater rim, and if you still have enough energy, another three to walk completely round it. It's slightly easier to walk counter-clockwise. In places, the inside walls of the volcano are almost vertical; certainly not a place for those who suffer from vertigo.

The ordinary mortal, however, will have been content with the view of Mount Longonot from afar and proceeded to the lakeshore, probably at the **Lake Naivasha Hotel**. Lake Naivasha's delight is its huge and varied bird population; well over 400 species have been recorded. On the lake itself, pink-backed pelicans, long-tailed cormorants, black crake, purple gallinules and jacanas, or lily-trotters, are all plentiful and easy to see, especially if a boat is hired from the hotel. A boat trip to look at birds can easily be combined with a visit to **Crescent Island**, where some wildlife roams free and you can experience the thrill of getting close to game on foot. You should keep a safe distance from male waterbuck, but the remaining game presents no danger. Your boatman will also take you to where hippo can be seen.

The central 'White' Highlands, north of the Aberdares

Ngong races

Not far from Lake Naivasha is **Hell's Gate National Park**. Access is from the Moi South Road, about ten kilometres (six miles) after the Lake Naivasha Hotel. Since there are no dangerous animals (so they say), walking in this park is allowed. Its interest lies in its solitude and its spectacular scenery. There are some plains game, and birders will be excited to know that this is one of the few places where nesting lammergeyers can be seen. Within the park is a geothermal station, the largest in Africa, and destined to provide—in time—the major part of Kenya's electricity needs. A day out to Lake Naivasha and Hell's Gate is very rewarding.

Another, and different day out is a safari to **Olorgesailie**, a prehistoric hunters' camp 65 kilometres (40 miles) from Nairobi, all on tarmac roads, save the last two kilometres. Leave Nairobi by the Magadi Road, which borders the western side of the Nairobi National Park. The road climbs over the slopes of the **Ngong Hills** with spectacular views over the Great Rift Valley, into which you descend on the way to this prehistoric gem. The site is well excavated and well laid out, and a knowledgeable guide is available. As well as a variety of fossilized bones of prehistoric creatures, the tools and weapons of the hunters lie around in incredible numbers. There is a small 'museum', a shelter for picnics, and a number of grass thatched huts for renting. Olorgesailie can be extremely hot, so go well prepared with drinks and sun hats.

Another possibility, which is also not in the tour operator's repertoire, is a visit to the tea and coffee growing areas in the **Limuru** district. Both these crops are interesting to see under cultivation, and if you stop at one of the many coffee or tea factories there will certainly be a welcome and an explanation of the processing procedures. Leave Nairobi on the Muranga road and pass the embassy area of Muthaiga. From Muthaiga the route to Gigiri (where the United Nations Environment Programme is based) is well signposted. Pass the entrance to UNEP, staying on the main Limuru road for some five kilometres (three miles) until there is a right-hand turn and a forest of signboards. Although none of these read 'coffee and tea', take this road, which climbs through local smallholdings where the principal crop seems to be bananas. Carry on for another five kilometres and you reach the coffee plantations, where you can stop and have a look around. Another five kilometres brings you into the tea growing areas, a sight as pretty as any landscape in Kenya. At the upper limits of the coffee you will have passed the **Kentmere Club**, a fine place to stop for lunch.

Not long after entering the tea plantations there is a right turn marked by another batch of signboards. If one of these indicates Limuru Girls School, you are on the right track. Take this route and wander through the lime-green countryside. After a few kilometres you will come to a small forest stretching on either side of the road. A troop of colobus monkeys lives here, which with a little patience you should be able to spot. When you reach the T-junction turn right and head back towards Nairobi. After eight kilometres (five miles), you reach a crossroads where you should turn left, heading for Kiambu. This is a smooth highway until you reach the bumps that signify arrival at another T-junction, where you turn right. After a few hundred metres you find another T-junction and, again, you turn right. Stay on this road to the centre of Nairobi, 12 kilometres (eight miles) away.

Those staying in Nairobi and looking for places to visit may notice 'Ol **Doinyo Sapuk**' (or Ol Donyo Sabuk) **National Park** shown on their map. There is no problem in reaching the park and returning in one day, but the roads within the park, although advertised as passable for saloon cars, are best tackled with a four-wheel-drive vehicle. *Ol Doinyo Sapuk* is Maa for the 'Hill of the Buffalo', and even now there are said to be plenty of buffalo in the forested slopes, but the real reward of a visit is the scenery. On a good day the summit takes in splendid views of Kilimanjaro, Mount Kenya and the Aberdares. For those interested in plants, attractions to look for are Afro-Alpine species such as giant lobelia, which are normally associated with the higher mountains.

The road to the park passes very close to **Fourteen Falls**, a dramatic series of waterfalls, particularly in the rainy season. The park is reached by taking the dual carriageway from Nairobi to Thika, but continuing on the Thika–Garissa road that by-passes the town. (Despite any curiosity aroused by the book *The Flame Trees of*

Thika, Thika is best left to its inhabitants.) Twenty kilometres (13 miles) from Thika a signboard directs drivers to the park. The Fourteen Falls Motel is on this corner. One kilometre down this road you come to a T-junction; turn left and shortly afterwards you will see a signboard indicating another left turn to Fourteen Falls. Less than a kilometre down this track is a clearing where you can park your car. Take everything valuable with you when you walk the short distance to the falls, and if there is a policeman on duty, feel relieved. If there isn't, there is likely to be a local person offering to guard your (now empty) car. You should accept his offer and tip him on your return—if your hub caps are still all there.

To continue to the park, return to the road you left when you turned down the track to the falls and turn left, crossing a series of bridges over the Athi River shortly afterwards. There is a great deal of birdlife around these bridges and you may wish to stop to look at the waterbirds and waders. Less than two kilometres (one mile) after the bridges, turn right at a dilapidated trading centre and you will reach the park gates in another two kilometres.

On the way to the summit you will come across three graves. These belong to Sir William Northrup McMillan, his wife, and their servant (for 75 years), Louise Decker. McMillan, a wealthy American, was host to ex-President Teddy Roosevelt when the latter made his celebrated big game hunting safari to Kenya in 1904. McMillan, knighted by the British for his charitable work during the First World War, owned the land that is now the national park and later bequeathed it to the nation. Perhaps that is the reason why no park entry fees are currently (in 1991) being levied. Sir William (the National Parks sign points to 'Lord McMillan's Grave') was all of 165 kilograms (365 pounds), with a 1.57-metre (62-inch) swordbelt, which accounts for the location of his grave—despite his expressed wish to be buried on the summit.

You may think that with all these things to do in and around Nairobi, there is no need to go on safari. You would be quite wrong, however, because Kenya's more than 50 parks and reserves provide such a variety of splendid attractions that you would certainly be missing something by ignoring them.

Kenya's National Parks and National Reserves

A national park differs from a national reserve in Kenya not because of its touristic importance, not in its relative wealth or lack of wildlife, not in its scenic splendour but merely because of ownership. The land in a national park belongs to the state and is administered by the central government, while the land in a national reserve belongs to a county council and is administered by that council (which in some cases delegates this responsibility to the central authorities). The Kenya Wildlife Service is the government's relevant administrative arm. There are 51 parks and reserves. Some of these are marine, but the majority are on land and occupy a huge area of the country. Often wildlife is in competition with humans, either because the land used for parks could equally well be suitable for human habitation, or because wild animals leave the parks and eat or destroy neighbouring crops. Some reserves are surrounded by a 'conservation or dispersal area', where wildlife and domestic animals co-exist and where the inhabitants have accepted some controls over the use and development of their land in exchange for a share in the revenue from the adjacent park or reserve.

The following list shows all the gazetted national parks and reserves in Kenya. In addition to these, there are areas protected from human encroachment by local ordinance (for example, the Maralal Game Sanctuary), areas protected as forest reserves, others protected under the *National Monuments and Antiquities Act*, and even a small area in Machakos district (Mutomo) where a number of unique plants can be found.

National Parks	Area Square Kms	National Reserves	Area Square Kms
1. Nairobi	117	Marsabit	1,132
2. Tsavo (East & West)	20,872	Shimba Hills	192
3. Mt Kenya	590	Lake Bogoria	107
4. Aberdare	766	Shaba	239
5. Meru	870	Kora	1,787
6. Ol Doinyo Sapuk	18	Masai Mara	1,510
7. Mt Elgon	169	Arawale	533
8. Sibiloi	1,570	Mwea	68
9. Saiwa Swamp	2	Rahole	1,270
10. Amboseli	392	Tana River	169

Uaso Nyiru River, Samburu, with Phoenix reclinata *trees*

14. Lake Nakuru	188	Dodori	877
15. Marsabit	360	South Kitui	1,833
16. Ruma	120	North Kitui	745
17. Hell's Gate	68	Bisanadi	606
18. Ndeere Island	4	South Turkana	1,091
19. Kisite Marine	28	Nasalot	92
20. Watamu Marine	10	Kerio Valley	66
21. Mombasa Marine	10	Kamnarok	877
22. Malindi Marine	6	Kakamega	447
23. Malindi Marine	213	Samburu	165
24. Mombasa Marine	200	Longonot	52
25. Kiunga Marine	250	Buffalo Springs	131
26. Mpunguti Marine	11	Laikipia	165

Planning a safari is not just a question of choosing the parks that take your fancy and setting off; it involves instead a major logistical exercise before a single animal can be seen. Distances are often huge, certainly by European standards, so backtracking proves time-wasting and expensive. For this reason, tour operators have developed what are known in the trade as 'circuits'. If you choose a safari offered by a tour operator—which most people do—it will consist of one or more circuits. Although the circuits do not have names, they can be described by compass directions so, for example, there is the south and southeastern circuit, which includes Amboseli and the two Tsavos. This circuit can start from either Mombasa or Nairobi, but in both cases you have to return to one of the points of origin in order to continue with another leg of the safari.

The central circuit heads northwards out of Nairobi and includes one of the three 'tree hotels' in the Mount Kenya region before continuing on to Nanyuki and the Mount Kenya Safari Club and thence to Samburu.This circuit backtracks as far as Isiolo and then returns to Nairobi via Meru National Park or crosses the top of the Aberdare Range to Lake Baringo or to pick up the Mara circuit at Nakuru.

The Mara circuit, which starts at Nairobi, first travels to Lake Naivasha and thence to Nakuru (or possibly an excursion to Lake Nakuru from Naivasha) and then to the famed Masai Mara. Returning from the Mara, the route backtracks to Lake Naivasha and then heads south to the capital.

The western circuit centres on Kisumu, a port on Lake Victoria. This can be reached from the Masai Mara but it is not the recommended route. The first stop on the western circuit could also be Lake Nakuru, continuing on the trans-Africa highway to Kisumu, a journey of about 195 kilometres (122 miles). From Kisumu the circuit takes in the Kakamega Forest, the Mount Elgon National Park, and possibly

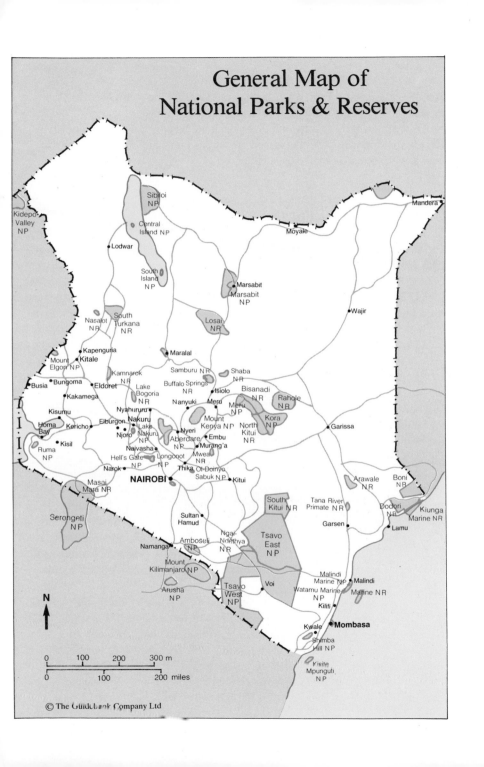

General Map of
National Parks & Reserves

Mandera

Kidepo
Valley
NP

Sibiloi
NP

Central
Island NP

Moyale

Lodwar

South
Island
NP

Marsabit
Marsabit
NP

Wajir

Nasalot
NR

South
Turkana
NR

Losai
NR

Kapenguria

Maralal

Mount
Elgon NP

Kitale

Kamnarok
NR

Samburu NR

Shaba
NR

Busia

Bungoma

Eldoret

Lake
Bogoria
NR

Buffalo Springs
NR

Isiolo

Bisanadi
NR

Rahole
NR

Kakamega

Nanyuki

Meru

Meru
NP

Kisumu

Nyahururu

Elburgon

Nakuru

Mount
Kenya NP

North
Kitui
NR

Kora
NP

Garissa

Homa
Bay

Kericho

Lake
Nakuru
NP

Nyeri

Embu

Kisil

Njoro

Aberdare
NR

Murang'a

Ruma
NP

Naivasha

Hell's Gate
NP

Longonot
NP

Mwea
NR

Narok

Thika

Ol-Doinyo
Sabuk NP

Kitui

NAIROBI

Arawale
NR

Boni
NR

Masai
Mara NR

South
Kitui NR

Tana River
Primate NR

Dodori
NR

Kiunga
Marine NR

Serongeti
NP

Sultan
Hamud

Garsen

Lamu

Namanga

Amboseli
NP

Ngai-
Ndethya
NR

Tsavo
East
NP

Mount
Kilimanjaro NP

Malindi
Marine NP

Malindi

Voi

Watamu Marine
NP

Marine NR

Arusha
NP

Tsavo
West
NP

Kilifi

Kwale

Mombasa

Shimba
Hill NP

N

Kisite
Mpunguti
NP

0	100	200	300 m

0		100		200 miles

© The Guidebook Company Ltd

Saiwa Swamp National Park, before turning eastwards for the return over Kenya's most scenic highway via Eldoret and Kabarnet to Lake Baringo.

These are the main circuits, and they include all the principal parks and reserves. The adjective 'principal' does not bestow any recognition other than to indicate that these seven sanctuaries are the most visited.

Nairobi National Park

The first of these seven is the **Nairobi National Park**. Created from a 'commonage' in 1945, 12 years after it had first been mooted by the then Game Warden of Kenya, Captain Archie Ritchie, the area had a troubled history. In two world wars it was used as a military backyard, where as many as 8,000 troops lived and trained. Puzzled visitors today see signs indicating 'Lone Tree', where there is no tree. This was the site of a bombing range in the Second World War.

All the Nairobi tour operators offer a three-hour tour to the park, but this is generally in the afternoon, though the best time for a visit is in the early morning. If you are pre-planning your visit to Kenya with a tour operator, build in a dawn trip. This will not only be rewarding in terms of game, but it will start your indoctrination into early rising, a feature of life on safari. The park has an area of highland forest where among the crotons, olives and cape chestnuts, you can search for bushbuck, monkeys and leopard. There is also a much larger area of open plains studded with acacia trees, where you will find Thomson's and Grant's gazelles, the common zebra, wildebeest, kongoni and warthog. The king of the beasts' domain is also here. Lions are among the laziest of creatures, so you are most likely to find them in the prone position. In the early morning they may well come out of the bush in which they have spent the night, choose a patch of high ground and bask in the warmth of the first hour of sun. If you are lucky enough to see cheetah, this will also be on the plains. Since cheetahs use their speed to kill they have little use for cover, except to escape the hot sun, and choose a vantage point such as a termite mound to survey their territory and locate prey.

The plains along the northern boundary of the park, where it borders the Nairobi-Mombasa road, are speckled with a chest-high acacia commonly called 'whistling thorn'. If you stop your car and there is any wind at all, you can hear it whistle as it passes over holes made by ants in the tree's galls. The tree is *Acacia drepanolobium*. Heading east over the plains you will encounter some small, man-made dams; these are usually worth a pause to view the birdlife attracted to the water. Eventually, you reach the richly forested banks of the Athi River, where tall yellow-barked acacias

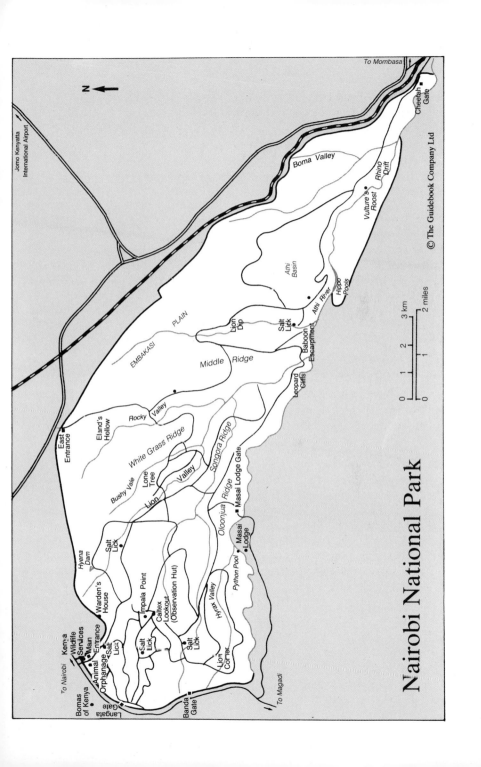

Nairobi National Park

© The Guidebook Company Ltd

To Mombasa

Cheetah Gate

Boma Valley

Rhino Drift

Vulture's Roost

Athi Basin

Hippo Pools

Athi River

Salt Lick

Baboon Escarpment

Lion Dip

EMBAKASI PLAIN

Middle Ridge

Leopard Cliffs

Rocky Valley

Eland's Hollow

White Grass Ridge

Songora Ridge

East Entrance

Bushy Vale

Lone Tree

Lion Valley

Oloonjua Ridge

Masai Lodge Gate

Masai Lodge

Hyena Dam

Salt Lick

Python Pool

Warden's House

Impala Point

Caltex Lookout (Observation Hut)

Hyrax Valley

Kenya Wildlife Services Main Entrance

Salt Lick

Salt Lick

Salt Lick

Animal Orphanage

Lion Corner

Banda Gate

Bomas of Kenya

Langata Gate

To Nairobi

To Magadi

Jomo Kenyatta International Airport

N

0   1   2   3 km

0   1   2 miles

Hippo showing his tonsils; there are Hippo Pools in Nairobi National Park

abound. These are *Acacia xanthophloea*, Kipling's fever tree, since they almost always grow in the presence of water. At the 'Hippo Pools' you can safely walk along the river bank and look for crocodile and, of course, hippopotamus. These two huge creatures get along with one another quite well; as is usual, it is man who is their greatest enemy. There was a time, just after the Second World War, when crocodile were killed in their thousands by commercial hide-hunters. Dr Hugh Cott writes that 60,000 were shot in 1954 alone, throughout East Africa. The slaughter ceased only when numbers were so reduced that the trade was no longer economically viable.

You may not see much of the hippos because they rarely leave the water during daylight. But since hippos cannot remain submerged for longer than four minutes, you will certainly see their nostrils, and probably their eyes and ears as well, just breaking the surface. They look quite equine, reflecting the Greek origin of the word 'hippopotamus', which means water horse.

Heading west from the Hippo Pools you pass through some of the prettiest scenery in the park. This is an area of steep valleys created by streams joining the Mbagathi River, the park's southern boundary. Here you will see baboon, vervet monkeys, waterbuck and hyrax. The sharp-eyed visitor may spot the mountain reedbuck and the even more elusive klipspringer. On the plains that stretch north you should find black rhino.

Enjoying the kill, Masai Mara

There are now more than 50 rhinos in Nairobi National Park, having been trans-located there for safety in the 1980s, when poaching in the remoter parts of the country was rife. The largest living bird in the world, the ostrich, is also common on these plains.There are other large birds that you may also see, notably kori bustard, crowned crane, marabou stork, black-headed heron and the Egyptian goose, a friendly, but noisy bird that you will find in almost all the parks.

Looking across the river that forms the southern boundary you will see the Kitengela Plains, which form a dispersal area for many of the park's ungulates. In the wetter months of the year, while water still stands in natural pools, the majority of the zebra and the wildebeest are found outside the park. In September, when the plains have dried out, the park hosts a mini-migration. It is quite the best time of year to visit. But at no time will you be disappointed, for in this 117 square kilometres (46 square miles) there are well over 80 species of mammals and more bird species than are found, for example, in the whole of the British Isles.

The Animal Orphanage, which is located near the main gate, is more of a zoo than a home for the lost and lame, and may not appeal to people who fail to see the reason for caging animals within sight and sound of a natural wildlife sanctuary. A more interesting experience may be a visit to Daphne Sheldrick's home on the other side of the park (near the Banda Gate on the Magadi Road), where she cares for young elephants and rhinos. Visitors are allowed in after 4 pm, and a donation is expected.

WILDLIFE CONSERVATION

By Nehemiah Rotich

The conservation of wildlife as an active pursuit in itself is relatively new in East Africa. However, the presence of wildlife as a vital resource is closely associated with the historical and economic development of the region.

East Africa secured a place for itself in modern history in the 11th century, when ivory was being exported from its coast by the Arabs—mainly from Mombasa, Tanga and Dar-es-Salaam. As the demand for ivory grew, the hunting of elephants spread inland. By the 19th century the abundance of wildlife was providing recreation, meat, trophies and ivory for the European settlers. In a number of cases, wildlife also menaced the settlers: some tried to eliminate entire populations of the offending animals; others sought a more rational approach by keeping certain areas as national parks and reserves. It is thanks to the latter's efforts that we have today's game parks and reserves, which form the principal areas of wildlife conservation in East Africa.

Kenya is one of the countries leading the drive for wildlife conservation in Africa. Before independence, wildlife interests had been placed under two bodies: the Board of the National Parks Trustees, and the Game Department. The former was charged with the administration of wildlife parks, while the Game Department managed and regulated hunting.

After independence in 1963, Kenya kept the two wildlife management bodies under the Ministry of Tourism or, for a while, under the Ministry of Environment and Natural Resources. In 1976, the government amalgamated the Board of National Parks Trustees and the Game Department to form the Wildlife Conservation and Management Department (WCMD), which was headed by a director and placed under the Ministry of Tourism and Wildlife. In January 1990, WCMD was turned into the Kenya Wildlife Service (KWS), a parastatal body also headed by a director. In addition to the new ministry, the Ministry of Environment and Natural Resources and the Ministry of Livestock Development play supplementary roles in the conservation of wildlife by managing the forests and rangelands—vital habitats for wildlife outside the gazetted conservation areas. Apart from these, a permanent presidential commission is charged with attending to issues of soil erosion, protection of water catchments, and re-afforestation.

Kenya's wildlife conservation policy is to be found in sessional paper 13

of 1973, in which the government issued a statement on the future of wild-life conservation in Kenya. Among the issues it covered are the following:
- Administration and financing of the wildlife service
- Functions of the wildlife service
- Protection and management of national parks and reserves
- Consumptive utilization of wildlife.

Kenya's custodian for wildlife is Kenya Wildlife Service. KWS's major objectives are to achieve wildlife habitat conservation, sustainable utilization of the wildlife resources, and the protection of people and their property from injury or damage by wild animals. KWS manages some 50 national parks and reserves, including marine parks and rhino sanctuaries, under three principal policy-drives: a nationwide system plan that states national policies; management plans that prescribe how individual parks and reserves are to be managed for periods of up to five years or more; annual plans prepared each year for the park wardens.

Kenya is also signatory to the following conventions (KWS being the executive body):
- African Convention on the Conservation of Nature and Natural Resources (Algiers, 1968). Kenya was one of the first countries to deposit instruments of ratification, along with Upper Volta (Burkina Faso), Swaziland and Ghana.
- Convention on International Trade in Endangered Species of Wild Fauna and Flora (CITES). Kenya was instrumental in the imposition of a ban on the international ivory trade in 1989. She has played an active role at CITES meetings.
- Convention of Wetlands of International Importance, especially Waterfowl Habitat (Ramsar Convention). Lake Nakuru with its famous flamingos has been placed on the list of wetlands of international importance.
- International Convention for the Regulation of Whaling.

Several non-governmental organizations complement the KWS's work on conservation in Kenya. The oldest of them is the East African Wild Life Society, originally founded as the Kenya Wild Life Society in 1956, along with its counterpart, the Wild Life Society of Tanganyika. The society's formation was deemed necessary because of the uncontrolled hunting and poaching of various animal species during the early and mid-1900s. The purpose of the society was to give public backing to the Trustees of the Kenya National Parks, the Game Department, and the wild animals under their protection. The society also aimed to provide a forum for discussing conservation issues while monitoring the performance of government in wildlife conservation. In 1961, the Wild Life Societies of Kenya and Tanganyika were amalgamated; they were joined by wildlife enthusiasts in Uganda to form the East African Wild Life Society, with the presidents of the three East African republics serving as joint patrons. Since its founding, membership has increased steadily and today there are some 10,000 members all over the world.

Originally, the efforts of the society were concentrated on the larger game species such as the elephant, leopard, lion, cheetah and rhino, which were the targets of the big game hunters. At this time, little attention was paid to the smaller species such as antelope, birds and butterflies. Nevertheless, over the years the society came to the realization that success could not be achieved through wildlife conservation alone. In order to preserve wildlife, its habitats must be preserved as well. Hence, the current objective of the society is 'to safeguard wildlife and its habitat in all its forms, as a national and international resource'.

It is becoming increasingly clear that governments in developing countries are unable to shoulder the entire burden of development and conservation. The demands for funds are simply too heavy. Thus governments have come to welcome assistance from various NGOs. Assistance from the Wild Life Society not only comes in the form of financial support, but also through the generation of public support for government projects. In this manner the society takes some pressure off the various East African governments. By the same token, the society can also apply pressure if government projects are not being carried out. The society thereby works as a monitoring group, criticizing governments if their jobs are done poorly and giving praise where it is due.

The standing committee examines and funds proposals received by the society. Since it is comprised of local experts, it is able to to establish policies and formulate its own proposals. The work performed by the

Amboseli with its many elephants is an ideal location for elephant research

society falls into five basic categories:

Conservation education This long-term project, equally important in the short term, is aimed at educating the peoples of East Africa about the wealth, both economic and cultural, of the wildlife that abounds in the region. Governments have apparently come to realize the importance of wildlife; however, wildlife cannot be effectively conserved until the people themselves see the value of the resource and the need for fuller cooperation with the authorities. The society sets aside a large proportion of its budget for the promotion of education and wildlife awareness. It supplies films and publications, and also finances the activities of the Wildlife Clubs of Kenya, Tanzania and Uganda, which now educate about 200,000 people.

Anti-poaching The society supports government anti-poaching units, mainly through the provision and servicing of vehicles, radio communication equipment, and the servicing of aircraft. Funds have also been provided to train personnel for this purpose.

Research The society allocates a great deal of its funds to research animals, plants and ecosystems. Surveys of many species, whether threatened or not, are funded in order to recommend the best conservation strategy. Many researchers are East African university students. Thus the society helps to train the local wildlife managers and ecologists of the future.

Animal Rescue Sometimes referred to as translocation, animal rescue is another activity funded by the society. It involves the relocation of threatened animals to a safer area, one of the ways in which the society can help to save a species threatened by agricultural encroachment, poachers, etc. For example, the society has been providing funds for the translocation of black rhinos to rhino sanctuaries, where they are protected from poachers and provided with safe breeding areas.

The society is delighted to welcome new members. For further details, write to the East African Wild Life Society, PO Box 20110, Nairobi.

Lake Nakuru National Park

Nakuru town is 156 kilometres (97 miles) from Nairobi and is reached by one of the best roads in Kenya. You leave the capital via Uhuru Highway, the wide dual carriageway that divides Nairobi in two. You will be following the old caravan route to Uganda, which used to be known as Slater's Road—after a captain in the Royal Engineers who first pioneered the route.

The road by-passes the small town of **Limuru**, famous for its Bata shoe factory and its misty cool weather. An alternative route out of Nairobi is via **Muthaiga**, the smartest of Nairobi's suburbs, and **Banana Hill**, the least smart. The bananas of that appropriately named trading centre soon yield to coffee and then you reach tea country, where you may stop and enjoy the view. You will see the shoots containing 'two leaves and a bud', the only part of the bush used in producing 'made tea'. A cluster of signs on your right conceals All Saints Church, a few yards from the road, in whose graveyard the celebrated anthropologist, Dr Louis Leakey, is buried.

Quite soon, you reach the township of Limuru, bustling and distinctly unattractive, its most noticeable feature being the huge number of *matatus* that line the main road. You join the Nairobi-Nakuru highway a few kilometres after leaving the town. The route from now on is pretty, passing first through smallholdings and patches of forest before these yield to spectacular views of the Great Rift Valley. There are a number of viewpoints beside the road where you can photograph the volcano-studded floor of the rift and be exposed to the high-powered salesmanship of the local curio vendors. **Lake Naivasha** is easily identified by its proximity to Mount Longonot, an extinct volcano 2,776 metres (9,110 feet) high. The road continues high above the valley floor passing **Lake Elementeita**, privately owned and often decorated with pink flamingos. At the northern end of this small lake a great battle took place in 1881 between the Wa-Kwavi, a once powerful and numerous section of the Masai, and a large Swahili caravan. The fight lasted all day until the Swahilis ran out of ammunition and retreated.They were followed and annihilated. Only three out of the caravan of 300 lived to relate the tale.

Just after Elementeita is a prehistoric site, **Kariandusi**, found in 1928 by Dr Leakey, which contains interesting examples of the distinctive Stone Age tools of Aechulean industry. There are also some examples of fossilized remains of the giant animals that characterized the Middle Pleistocene period.

Another 30 kilometres (19 miles) brings you to **Nakuru town**, whose colonnaded shops in the main street will suggest a film set for a Western. Nairobi often boasts that its proximity to a national park is unique, but in fact Nakuru is even nearer to a national park than the capital. From the very centre of the town you descend no more

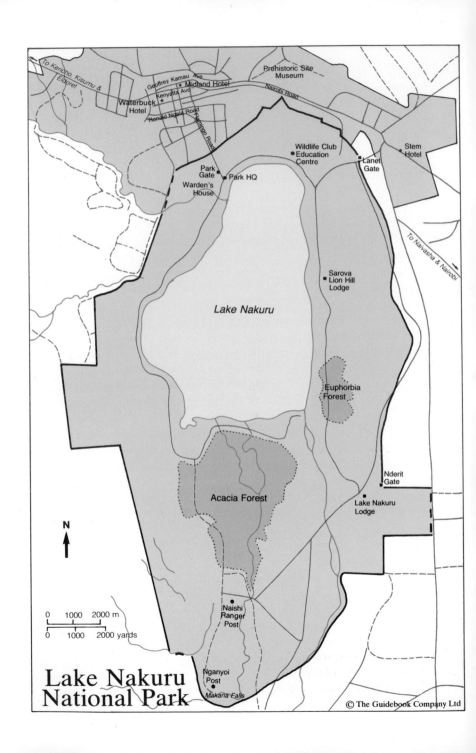

To Kericho, Kisumu & Eldoret

Geoffrey Kamau Ave
Midland Hotel

Kenyatta Ave

Waterbuck Hotel

Ronald Ndala Road

Flamingo Road

Prehistoric Site Museum

Nairobi Road

Wildlife Club Education Centre

Lanet Gate

Stem Hotel

Park Gate

Park HQ

Warden's House

To Naivasha & Nairobi

Sarova Lion Hill Lodge

Lake Nakuru

Euphorbia Forest

Nderit Gate

Acacia Forest

Lake Nakuru Lodge

N

Naishi Ranger Post

| 0 | 1000 | 2000 m |
| 0 | 1000 | 2000 yards |

Nganyoi Post

Makaria Falls

Lake Nakuru
National Park

© The Guidebook Company Ltd

than a couple of kilometres through dusty streets, before you reach the park gates, at an altitude of 1,758 metres (5,767 feet).

Lake Nakuru National Park has recently been enlarged, firstly because its very existence was threatened by sewage pollution from the town, and secondly to provide a sanctuary for black rhino. The latter undertaking has necessitated a fence—to keep out poachers rather than to restrict the movements of wildlife. There are now about 25 rhino in the park, one of the largest concentrations in the country. But the main reason for visiting Lake Nakuru must be to see the world-famous flamingos, lesser and greater—several thousand more of the former than of the latter. All manner of superlatives have been used to describe the vast numbers of flamingo that turn the turgid waters of the lake a brilliant fuschia pink. Lake Nakuru and the other alkaline lakes of Kenya and Tanzania support between three and four million lesser flamingo. These spectacular aggregations feed on the microscopic algae that abounds in these foul waters.

Flamingo have wonderfully specialized adaptations that enable them to crop the algae. When feeding, the flamingo submerges its bill, upside down, in the top five centimetres of the water. A circular tongue that fits neatly in the lower mandible acts as a piston, sucking in and forcing out water. Inside the bill are rows of hairy processors that lie down when the water is sucked in and stand erect as the water tries to leave. The algae is filtered to the side of the bill, where it collects in masses on downy hairs, whence it is transferred to the tongue and then to the gullet in the same piston action that brings water into the bill. Thus these minute plants are consumed in sufficient quantities, as a sort of soup, to nourish and sustain the bird. It is estimated that an average population of flamingo on Lake Nakuru harvests about 250,000 kilogrammes of algae per hectare (101 tonnes per acre) per year. The greater flamingo feed farther out into the lake than the lesser, and do not harvest the blue-green algae but eat small crustacea and the larvae of lake flies. The greater flamingo can be recognized not only by its greater size (it is some 40 centimetres, or 16 inches, taller) but also by its bill, which is pink compared with the deep carmine of the lesser.

The lake is extremely rich in other birdlife. At times, little grebes occur in their thousands as do the white-wing black terns, winter migrants that seem not to discriminate between the alkaline and the freshwater lakes. Of the ducks, the Cape wigeon is plentiful (and only found on alkaline lakes), and the maccoa can be easily recognized by its habit of swimming low in the water and (in the case of the male) by a cobalt-blue bill. Two of the many fish-eating birds that cannot be missed are the pelican and the cormorant. Both are recent arrivals, for until recently there were no fish in Lake Nakuru. In the early 1960s, a diminutive species of tilapia (much prized food fish common in Lake Victoria and other freshwater lakes of East Africa), *Tilapia grahami*, was introduced into Nakuru and has been able to survive both the alkalinity and the high water temperature. It now forms the diet of a large number of birds, including darters, grebes, storks, fish eagles, ibis, spoonbills and several species of herons.

Over 400 species of birds have been recorded in the park, the majority of these away from the lake. Around the lake itself is an expanse of smelly mud on which almost nothing will grow. However, there are patches of a spiky grass, *Sporobolus spicatus*, especially on the eastern side of the lake, although nothing eats it. The dramatic vistas that this absence of vegetation creates are more than adequate compensation for the not so attractive smells. Local birders participate in bird ringing, or banding, a matter of some significance as the lake is a very important wintering area or stopover place for migrant birds from a large area of Eurasia. Rings provide evidence that the birds return to the very same place year after year. A ruff, ringed at Lake Nakuru, was shot three months later at Yakutsk, on the Lena River in Siberia.

But this is not just a park for bird enthusiasts; other forms of wildlife are numerous. In the beautiful acacia woodlands that surround much of the lake there are many waterbuck. Two species of waterbuck are found in Kenya, and Nakuru boasts the less prevalent defassa (*Kobus defassa*), with its noble bearing and an entirely white rump that distinguishes it from the common waterbuck (*Kobus ellipsiprymnus*). There are several thousand waterbuck in this small park, an indication of the lack of predators both animal and human. Despite their rather strong smell (of turpentine), waterbuck are preyed upon by lion and leopard, which kill the females and the young. The males have horns but their main defence is to take to water to escape their attackers. They are excellent swimmers.

Along the lake edge you may come across a near relative of the waterbuck: the reedbuck. This is the bohor reedbuck, which is usually seen singly or in pairs and is easily distinguished by its uniformly red sand colour and, in males, its forward-curved horns. Olive baboon are also common in the yellow-barked acacia woodland, their baleful expression belying their intelligence but not their ferocity.

Apart from the rhino, which is the park's most important attraction after the flamingo, there is another species to look for: Rothschild's giraffe, a small number of which live in the southwest part of the park. Translocated to Nakuru from farmland in western Kenya just in time to avoid extinction, the Rothschild's (sometimes called the Baringo giraffe) is said to have five horns. In some individuals it is possible to see two protuberances in line with the ears, but Rothschild's giraffe is better identified by its noticeably pale colour, stocky build, and white 'socks'. If you see this giraffe you have seen one of the rarest animals in Africa, for not much hope is held out for the few that used to be found in northeastern Uganda, nor for those that were once plentiful in the southern Sudan.

Fish eagle

Red hornbill

Thomson's gazelle are plentiful, as are impala, while among the rarer antelopes you may spot the diminutive, and very graceful, steinbuck. This small creature is distinguished by his horns (only grown by the males), which are set nearly at right angles to the face and curved slightly forward at the tips. In the acacia woodland, look out for the shy bushbuck, and the tiny dikdik, which, like the steinbuck, has a conspicuous glandular patch in front of the eyes. In the trees are plenty of black-faced vervet monkeys. If you look carefully you may also locate colobus monkeys, which are harder to see as they do not congregate in such numbers as the vervets. If you get very close to a colobus you may notice an anatomical curiosity: the absence of a thumb.

The euphorbia forest, very easy to identify on the eastern side of the lake, is worth a few minutes study. There are about 150 indigenous species of euphorbia, of which about 20 are trees or shrubs. The Nakuru forest species is *Euphorbia candelabrum*, which grows to a height of 15 metres (48 feet). From its short, thick trunk a dense, crowded mass of candelabra-like branches ascend into a massive crown. All the euphorbias contain a sticky, milky latex that is often copious and almost always poisonous. The tree is a xerophyte, that is, it is fully adapted to growth under very dry conditions. Water is conserved by the absence of leaves, leading to only minor loss from transpiration. To compensate for the loss of leaves, the stems have developed four flanges or wings and this increased green surface area takes over the process of photosynthesis normally undertaken by leaves. This species, and indeed all euphorbias, must not be confused with the cactus family. There is only one true member of the cactus family in the whole of Africa, a forest epiphyte called *Rhipsalis*. All the other cacti that you may notice in gardens in Kenya have been introduced.

ACCOMMODATION

■ IN THE PARK
Lake Nakuru Lodge (120 beds, 2 stars)
Sarova Lion Hill (120 beds, 3 stars)

■ IN NAKURU TOWN
Waterbuck Hotel (150 beds, 2 stars)
Midland Hotel (63 beds, 2 stars)

Masai Mara National Reserve

The Mara, as the locals call it, is Kenya's finest game sanctuary. Really part of the Serengeti ecosystem, it is only a separate entity because the international border slices across that great wilderness, leaving the Serengeti in Tanzania and the Mara in Kenya. The Masai Mara National Reserve is administered by the Narok County Council, which staffs and maintains the reserve and collects the revenue earned. Currently, something less than 25 per cent of the revenue is returned to the Masai people, whose land is adjacent to the reserve. The remainder supports over 90 per cent of all the activities of the county council, clearly illustrating the very important role that tourism plays in the welfare of the local inhabitants.

The reserve's area is about 1,510 square kilometres (583 square miles), having been reduced by about 17 per cent in 1984. On the other hand, the dispersal area, where sound conservation practices are followed by the Masai, is much larger than the reserve itself. Wildlife can be just as abundant outside as inside, and there are more camps and lodges outside the reserve than within it. The abundance of game and its immense variety make the Mara the most sought after reserve in Kenya. It is probably the only park or reserve in the country where you can be certain to find the 'Big Five': elephant, buffalo, leopard, lion, and rhino.

In Maa, the language of the Masai, the word *Mara* alludes to something spotted. The undulating landscape is speckled with clumps of dense bush, which if viewed from the escarpment that forms the western boundary of the reserve, explains the local name. These bush thickets are mainly composed of the easily recognized *Croton dichogamus,* whose young leaves have a silvery underside but whose older leaves turn a rusty orange on the upper side. This dominating bush is plentiful because it is not much liked by any of the browsing animals, although baboon and impala are partial to its fruit. But the survival of vegetation is not just a matter of what is liked or not liked as food; it is more a combination of fire and elephant. Certainly, the relation between grassland and bush depends very much on the frequency and severity of fires. Some controlled burning takes place under the supervision of the warden but most fires are unwanted, and are started by Masai outside the reserve (just before the rains, they burn rank grass to encourage succulent new growth). Although most vegetation suffers from fire, the dominant grass of the plains, red oat grass, develops more strongly under repeated burning.

Elephant damage woodland by knocking down trees and by trampling new seedlings, but they also destroy grassland by pulling out grass by the roots. If you watch elephants eating on the plains, you will see that they grasp a tuft of grass with their trunk and then kick the base of the tuft to loosen the roots. In an area of high rainfall

(following pages) In the dry months, the wildebeest migration across the Mara River provides one of nature's greatest spectacles

like the Mara such destruction is not as serious as it is in, say, Amboseli, where the total environment is much more fragile.

There are now more elephants in the Mara than in living memory—well over 1,000—the resident population having been supplemented by those escaping poachers in the surrounding countryside and in Tanzania. Since rich woodland areas border the Mara River and to a lesser extent other rivers, particularly the Talek, elephant damage to these forested areas is now very serious. You may spot some patches of forest surrounded by electric fences, the latest attempt by environmental managers to stave off this destruction. But woodland and forest are but a small part of the Mara. Mostly, it is grassland. Some of the plains, particularly those to the north and west of Keekorok Lodge, are natural, which is to say that they exist on shallow soils overlying rock and are thus unable to support deep-rooted vegetation. Others are derived: meaning they have been created by fire, which has destroyed the bush, and by heavy grazing.

The grasses on the open plains are often short; indeed, you may hear these areas referred to as 'short grass plains', although that is a misleading description as they are kept short by continuous grazing during the growing period. If you look carefully you will see that these fine-leaved grasses often grow from little cushions that trap rainwater, even if it is slight. There are also considerable differences between day and night temperatures in the Mara and condensation occurs below ground. Botanists have found that the roots of many of the Mara grasses are specially adapted to make the best use of that moisture. As long as the grass remains green and growing, animals continue to graze on it. What is eaten by animals is soon replaced, and the grass continues to grow as long as it is grazed, in the same way that a lawn grows after mowing. Since the replacement takes time (about two weeks), the herds move around the plains, returning to the grazed parts as soon as re-growth has taken place. If the number of animals is not enough to keep the plains grazed down, the grass grows to maturity and flowers. In this state many of the plains' animals are unable to utilise the long grass; thus use begets use, and the longer the game can keep the grass growing and immature, the longer will be the productivity of the pasture.

Different species of animals have different grazing requirements. Zebra prefer the coarse long grass while Thomson's gazelle choose the tiny leaf shoots left after the larger animals have fed. This grazing succession means that different species of animals are zoned across the landscape. When growth stops after the end of the rainy season the grazing succession tends to become a grazing progression, with the herds moving in search of new pastures. The famous wildebeest migration is part of this progression.

Many people, when referring to the wildebeest migration, are thinking of that spectacular time when the enormous herds mass together and begin their trek. Unfor-

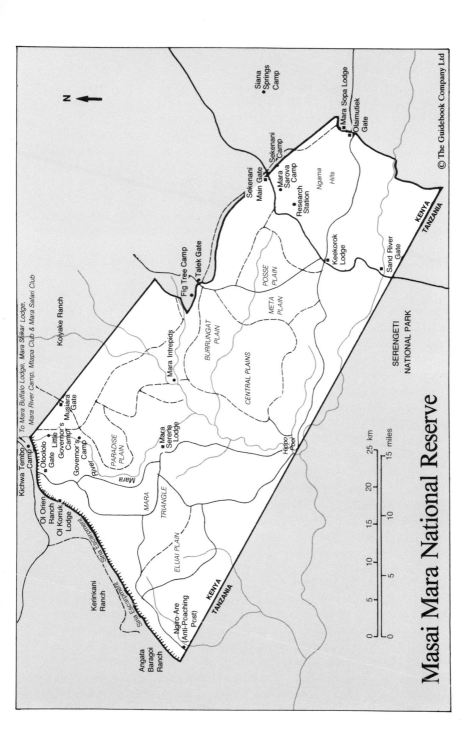

Masai Mara National Reserve

© The Guidebook Company Ltd

tunately, such moments are impossible to predict accurately as they depend on variable factors, such as weather and the availability of water and grazing. Nevertheless, the migration does follow a pattern, even if this varies from year to year.

The Serengeti ecosystem, of which the Mara forms the northern extension, occupies some 25,000 square kilometres (10,000 square miles). In this vast area live about 1,350,000 wildebeest, 500,000 Thomson's gazelle and 250,000 zebra. All these animals migrate, the gazelle covering less distance than the wildebeest or the zebra. In late May or early June, depending on the weather, the wildebeest herds move away from the short-grass plains in central Serengeti and disperse throughout the woodland areas of the western corridor and the northern part of the park towards the Kenya border. For the last 20 years or so this march northwards has extended, so that the herds now enter the Mara in late June or early July in search of the grazing that has been exhausted in the Serengeti.

In the 1950s, there were thought to have been around 300,000–400,000 wildebeest in the Serengeti, but in the second half of the 1960s and in the 1970s, this number dramatically increased to its present level. The Serengeti National Park has been unable to sustain this immense population explosion on its own. The wildebeest enter the Mara in the company of large numbers of zebra, although it is not clear whether the zebra lead the wildebeest or vice-versa. However, the Thomson's gazelle that have accompanied the migration from the southern part of the Serengeti across the central plains do not move into the bushland in the western corridor or move northwards to Kenya. About 500,000 of Serengeti's wildebeest population enter the Mara and stay until late October. They are joined by another 100,000 or so from the Loita Hills in Kenya, which also enter the Mara during the dry months to take advantage of the abundance of succulent grasses. In the second half of their stay in the Mara the wildebeest plunge in huge columns across the Mara River into the 'Mara Triangle', providing one of nature's greatest spectacles. But travelling among these huge, amorphous herds during the four months in which they invade the Mara is also an astounding experience—and is made more exciting still by the huge number of predators attending on the herds.

After returning to the Serengeti, the migrating wildebeest reach the short grass plains in the south in time for the fresh green shoots brought on by the short rains. Soon after arrival, the calves are born, almost *en masse*. The herds stay on the short grass until the cycle begins again in April–May. Rutting takes place as the storm clouds of the long rains gather; the wildebeest's gestation takes 240 days, almost the whole of the period when the migration is taking place.

The plains of the Masai Mara are still filled with game, even when the migrating wildebeest are absent. Stopping your vehicle on Paradise Plains, for example, will give you a 360-degree view. You should be able to see Thomson's and Grant's gazelle, topi,

An 'ethereal' impala, Samburu

Topi, Masai Mara

Vignettes

Each animal has its characteristic behaviour as well as appearance and with every hour of watching you learn more of both. I used to think that the Creator designed man and the major animals Himself but contracted out the lesser creatures to competition among the angels, who showed varying degrees of taste.

Certainly the wildebeest is rather a pathetic effort. His is a sort of sham—he looks so fierce and is mild as a sheep; he seems built to charge, with his humped shoulders, and thick neck, yet I believe he is never known to do such a rude thing. He is so quaint that you feel he ought to be rare; yet he is so common that people hardly ever pay him the compliment of shooting him except for meat. He looks quite dignified standing and yet, when he starts to run, he can't even run straight, but wobbles from side to side, flirting his ridiculous tasselled tail. Also, one feels that any creature that looks as if he were related to buffalo and bison ought to have more proper pride than to consort with zebra.

For zebras are vulgar. I tried hard not to admit it as I wanted to admire them and think they were at least pretty. But they are so disgustingly, fatly prosperous-looking and so cheeky. I am not surprised to be told that their flesh is sickly and sweet. It looks like that. Their figures, not to put it grossly, are comfortable. They are so much like the roundest and tamest ponies that you feel they have no business to be idling about doing nothing. I might have forgiven them all this if it had not been for their buttocks. Their marking, if rather loud, is not without a certain charm, but on these parts it is larger as if it could not quite fit over the bulge and, nature's upholstery at fault, had to be stretched.

To turn from zebras to something I can praise unreservedly, let us talk of 'Tommies' (Thompson's gazelle). They are more beautiful even than the little dik-dik. In these animals that run clear in the light of the open plains, proportion counts most as an element of beauty. And the proportion of the Tommy is superb. I suppose he stands about 3 feet high at the head and the thin black horns the males carry are of a length and curve that completely satisfy. But the Tommy has more to commend him; his colour is of golden-red sand with a bold bar of black on his flanks and a belly and tail of snow.

He is curious without being really cheeky. And he is surely one of the happiest of God's creation; his jaunty little trot expresses contentment, while his tail wags as if in continuous delight. I need not say he is all grace and gentleness with his tiny cloven hoofs and fine limbs.

Much of this applies to the impala. But the impala touches a deeper range of feeling: the word 'ethereal' comes to mind, which would not occur to the best friend of the Tommy. I do not know the greater kudu well enough to generalize very certainly, though I saw him in Somaliland, but I would say that, of all buck I have seen, the impala is the most beautiful in proportions and actions. And colour! It is perhaps unwise to be so absolute in speaking of the colour of African creatures. They change in sun and shadow and in morning and evening. A change of position catching a new slant of light is enough to change brown to grey, or even black. But, mostly, the impala is the red-brown of the English fox, with no pattern, only a lightening of tone on quarters and breast. About twice as large as the Tommy, and less stocky, finer, with more curving lines, he carries his horns, not with the kingly, rather self-conscious pride Landseer shows in his stags, but with an airy unconsciousness. When you look worshipfully at this creature and clear your mind to accept what impression he will give, it is as much an emotion as an impression, a sense of the poetry of form and movement; his exquisite fragility has an element of pathos: he stands for that kind of beauty that seems hardly attached to the ugliness. Yet, when he moves, springing in nervous fashion high into the air in the middle of his stride, the impression changes a little, for you see that his fragile-seeming form is strong in bone and sinew, and that he, too, can express the joy of life, though it is still in more spiritual fashion than other gazelle. This spirituality is especially marked in the doe and with it a quality hard to name. The nearest word I can find—and it is one that has become tarnished—is meekness. But it is also femininity, the femininity of the world of nature, of the timid, the pursued, the gentle, who must accept their destiny without striving or crying, and who, in bearing their young in all the dangers of the open plains, are endowed, season by season, with that dignity that we read into motherhood among human beings.

Margery Perham, East African Journey

Coke's hartebeest, impala, zebra, and possibly elephant, buffalo, warthog, giraffe and eland. In May, June and November, these plains are often carpeted with a wild flower, *Cycnium tubulosum*, which is in fact a semi-parasite hosted by the roots of the surrounding grasses. There are two sub-species of this 'waste paper flower', one pink and one white. Another pretty post-rains wild flower is *Crossandra subacaulis*, easily identified by its delicate apricot colour.

Bushland occurs in small pockets, sometimes close enough together to afford cover for the rhino, of which there are more than 20 in the reserve. Rhino are territorial and mark their territories with dung heaps, which they scatter with their hind feet. The animals return regularly to resupply these heaps. Both male and female carry two horns, the front horn usually longer than the rear one but not necessarily so. Front horns have been measured at up to 119 centimetres (47 inches) and rear horns up to 53 centimetres (21 inches); the forest-dwelling rhino has longer horns than those of the plains. The male stands slightly higher than the female and weighs around two tonnes. Rhino spoor is one of the easiest to identify, since its three toes make a print like the ace of clubs. Rhino feed mainly at night, but also in the early morning and late evening, so these may be the best times to get a glimpse of this rare creature. During the heat of the day the animals lie down in shady places and are much more difficult to spot.

Elsewhere in the bushland, at the other end of the weight scale, you will certainly see the tiny dikdik, which weighs around three and a half kilograms (eight pounds) and is also territorial. Dikdik mate for life and do not drink water, obtaining their liquid needs from the food they eat. Another browser found in the bushland is the impala, probably Africa's most graceful antelope. This species is found in breeding herds of females and young, or in all-male groups numbering from ten to 50. These dominant males can be seen bringing up the rear of the female herds, easily spotted because of their horns, and ever ready to defend their mastery of the herd against the intrusions of impudent bachelors.

Although buffalo are grazers, they prefer to feed in forest and brush where there is shade and cover. So these herds, too, can be found in the bushland as well as on the plains, and are often divided into two: the mixed-sex breeding herd, and smaller groups of elderly animals. A large buffalo weighs around one and a half tonnes and with its enormous, heavily bossed horns, has no enemy to fear. A lion approaching a buffalo herd will almost certainly be driven away by the bulls, who form a defensive circle around the females and the calves.

The croton thickets are also hideouts of the elusive leopard, but not necessarily so, for leopard also frequent the forest areas and rocky promontories that give not only cover but panoramic views. Leopard hunt mainly at night and often carry their kill, in an extraordinary display of strength, high into a tree. So if you are in wood-

King of the jungle, Masai Mara

land or forest, don't neglect to scan the trees where a hanging tail often betrays the location of this shy animal. Their preferred prey is probably impala, although they kill a wide range of antelope as well as young zebra. Baboons and monkeys are also eaten but the legend that baboon and leopard are eternal enemies is more a product of the clamour raised when a group of baboons spot the predator. Leopards are loners, with males defending a territory and females their own home-range. They hunt over a wide area, generally staying in one area for only a short time before moving on, because their prey becomes increasingly vigilant when the marauder is in residence. Gestation lasts three months but the cubs are seldom seen, since they are hidden in caves or crevices by their protective mother.

Far less secretive, and therefore more frequently seen, is the cheetah, an inhabitant of the open plains. Taller and slimmer than the leopard with which it is often confused, the cheetah also has small, round, solid spots evenly distributed over its body, whereas the leopard's spots are clustered in rosettes on its shoulders and body. A less noticeable difference is that the leopard has fully retractable claws, while the cheetah has blunt and only partially retractable claws, very much like those of a dog. Cheetah (the word is Indian in origin) hunt by running down their prey at great speed. They can touch 100 kph (60 mph), but such speeds cannot be maintained for more than 200 to 300 metres. Their favourite prey in the Mara is Thomson's gazelle, but they also hunt hares, young warthog and even game birds. The male and female are similar, although the male is slightly larger and the small ruff, or crest, on its shoulder is more pronounced. Male cheetah are generally solitary but sometimes sibling groups of up to five are found together. Females, too, are solitary, although their cubs stay with them for over a year until they have learned to hunt and are ready to leave home. A litter is usually no more than four, although five and even six are not unknown. The survival rate is not high, however, with seldom more than one or two of a litter reaching maturity.

But the king of the jungle is also the king of the Mara; the reserve is world-famous for the number of its lion and for the magnificent black manes they carry. There are over 1,000 lion in the Mara, so they are not difficult to find. Family groups, or prides, can number as many as 30. One of nature's most endearing sights is to watch a bevy of cubs teasing their sleepy parents. Lions are the most indolent of all the Mara's creatures. Confident of their superiority, they slumber the day away, only raising their heads now and again to yawn or flick away a fly. But towards sundown the lionesses become alert, watching for possible prey and patiently weighing up the options. Of course males do hunt as well, but when part of a pride, they generally leave this chore to the females. Some say that the males stay in the background because their manes are conspicuous, but many male lions have only small manes or none at all, and these animals, too, seem quite content to let their females do the hunting. A more probable explanation is that the lioness is lighter, slimmer and faster than the male. Lions usually give birth once every two years. The litter of two to four cubs is dropped in tall, thick vegetation, where they remain until they are ready to join the pride some two months later.

You should almost certainly see another of the Mara's predators: the hyena. These curious creatures are most likely to be found in the vicinity of a lion kill, for although they are themselves excellent hunters, they are not averse to a little scavenging—nor, indeed, are any of the carnivores save the cheetah.

The spotted hyena has a complex social structure centering on a 'clan', a loose group numbering up to a hundred animals. Each clan occupies a territory and defends it against non-clan individuals. Usually hyena hunt alone but two or three hunting together can bring down a zebra or a wildebeest, and within minutes nothing remains save the horns and the jawbones. That is why seeing hyena on a kill is a rare event—that and the fact that hyena hunt mainly at night. Their 'whoop' of recognition is a common sound around the lodges at night, and their maniacal 'laughter' is a sure sign that a hunt is in progress or an unwanted interloper from another clan has been sighted. The young, usually two, are born in disused antbear holes, or nowadays in the concrete culverts under the park roads.

Biding its time and keeping just out of trouble, the jackal also waits for scraps from the king's table. Three species of jackal are found in the Mara but by far the most common is the black- or silver-backed, usually seen in pairs resolutely trotting towards an invisible destination. This determined trot is sometimes a signal that you are in the neighbourhood of a kill. If you are lucky enough to come across an actual lion hunt, the jackal's haunting wail, which signals success, is a sound that will remain with you always. Otherwise they are usually silent. The side-striped jackal, with a white tail tip, is not at all common in the Mara but is present and can be seen in wooded or open country. The golden jackal, not as glamorous as the name suggests, is also there, but is just as rare as his side-striped cousin.

The wild dog is the least common of all the larger carnivores. Sometimes called the 'Cape hunting dog' but now more frequently the African wild dog, this animal is becoming increasingly scarce, partly because of epidemic diseases and partly through the loss (to humans) of their traditional habitats. Packs of these dogs, which number from as few as two to as many as 40, hunt over very wide territories in all sorts of terrain except forest. They are determined and efficient killers and a wild dog hunt is a never-forgotten experience. The leader chooses his victim and the whole pack seems to be immediately aware of the potential prey. Two or three dogs lead the chase and as they tire, others who have followed less energetically take over the lead. As the

quarry tires, the pack closes in and eats it virtually alive.

Hunting dogs have up to 16 pups, which are born in shallow burrows or 'earths'. These smell disgusting (as do the dogs themselves). The arrival of pups is the most likely time for you to locate these animals, since the dogs cannot roam far while the litter is being weaned. As the puppies grow they venture farther from their earths to meet the returning hunters, whom they greet by pushing their noses into the older dogs' mouths, causing regurgitation of food for the puppies. Adult dogs also make use of this greeting behaviour pattern. There is not much chance of seeing hunting dogs within the reserve, but a pack is often in the northern dispersal area in the neighbourhood of Aitong. There is a research team in the Mara, which will be glad to hear from you if you have taken pictures of dogs in the Mara, or if you can relay information that might be useful to the team. There is a also project notebook in each lodge, in which you can record your observations.

There are several lesser carnivores in the Mara, some of which you may see even in the lodges or camps. The genet, which is nocturnal, visits some of the camps to be fed, and this is almost certainly the only chance the visitor has of seeing this lithe, long-bodied hunter. Although somewhat cat-like, the genet is related to the mongoose. It feeds on birds (particularly the roosting guinea fowl), reptiles, hares and insects. Four species of mongoose are found in the Mara and are predominantly diurnal (though the white-tailed mongoose is strictly nocturnal), so are quite frequently seen; in some camps they have set up home and seem quite fearless, even fond of tourists. In the Mara Intrepids Club there is a very large group of dwarf mongoose.

You should try to stay as long as possible in the Masai Mara, for not only is it scenically beautiful but its wide variety of wildlife, including birdlife, demand a lengthy stay. With more time you can become more discerning about your game-viewing. You can spend longer with a particular species and enjoy understanding its behaviour, or you can hunt for a particular animal, such as the small herd of roan antelope found in the southwestern corner of the reserve. You can also sample some of the other attractions, such as the hot-air balloons that fly every morning (except in May and June) from Keekorok, Governor's, Fig Tree, Serena and Sarova (although you don't have to stay in those lodges and camps to take a balloon ride). You can also fly by aircraft from any of the lodges to Rusinga Island, in Lake Victoria, for a morning's fishing, and bring back your catch to share with other visitors.

Masai mothers watch proudly as their warrior sons prepare for the head-shaving rite

ACCOMMODATION

■ IN THE MASAI MARA NATIONAL RESERVE

LODGES
Keekorok (153 beds, 4 stars)
Mara Serena (156 beds, 4 stars)
Mara Sopa (144 beds, 3 stars)—Mara Sopa is technically just outside the reserve, but access is through the reserve.

TENTED CAMPS AND TENTED LODGES
Mara Intrepids Club (50 beds, 3 stars)
Governor's Camp (72 beds, 2 stars)
Little Governor's (34 beds, 2 stars)
Mara Sarova (110 beds, 3 stars)

■ OUTSIDE THE MASAI MARA RESERVE

LODGES
Mara Shikar (180 beds, unclassified)
Ol Kurruk (38 beds, 4 stars).

An isolated manyatta *on the Masai plains*

TENTED CAMPS AND LODGES
Mara Safari Club (80 beds, 4 stars)
Fig Tree Camp (130 beds, unclassified)
Kichwa Tembo (80 beds, 2 stars)
Mara River Camp (52 beds, 2 stars)
Mara Buffalo (72 beds, 1 star)
Siana Springs (76 beds, unclassified)
Sekanani Camp (20 beds, unclassified)
Oseur Tented Camp (44 beds, unclassified)

Samburu

There are three national reserves making up the area generally known as Samburu. These are the **Samburu National Reserve**, **Shaba National Reserve** and **Buffalo Springs National Reserve**. In total, they cover an area of 535 square kilometres (206 square miles). Isiolo County Council administers both Shaba and Buffalo Springs, and Samburu County Council looks after Samburu. This division of responsibilities results in certain administrative differences, notably the different entry fees charged in the two districts. By agreement between the two councils, an entry ticket purchased in one council's area is valid in the other area on the same day on which it was issued.

The Samburu region is arid, harsh, and savagely beautiful. This is a place where you really feel you are in Africa. Most of the three reserves lie under 1,460 metres (4,000 feet) and are hot by day but cool by night. The average maximum temperature is around 30°C (86°F) and the minimum 20°C (68°F). Rain falls mainly in April, May and November but generally only in scattered showers, sometimes heavy.

The annual rainfall is 300–350 mm (12–14 inches). In most places the soil is extremely porous and rainwater disappears quickly. But even this small amount of rain is sufficient to mantle Samburu in the greenest of greens as the acacias throw out succulent, feathery, emerald leaves. In April, May and June *Delonix elata* blooms and its creamy wax-like flowers with long projecting stamens create a floral fantasy. This tree is a relative of the spectacular flamboyant, which flowers in scarlet-red profusion at the coast. At the same time of year the 'sausage tree', *Kigelia africana*, produces a multitude of pendant ox-blood red flowers. These impressive trees grow along the banks of the Uaso Ngiro River, which is the boundary between Samburu and Isiolo districts and the lifeline of the three reserves. *Uaso Ngiro* (variously *Uaso Nyiro* or *Ewaso Ngiro*) means 'brown river' in Maa, the Masai language that is also spoken by the Samburu people. The name derives, of course, from the colour of the soil brought

Samburu, Buffalo Springs and Shaba National Reserves

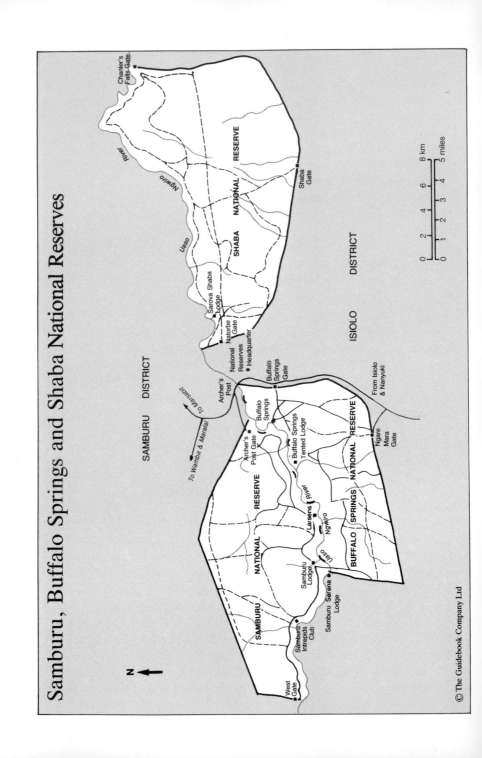

© The Guidebook Company Ltd

down from the highlands where the river originates. The river never reaches the sea but ends in a swamp in the torrid desert of northern Kenya. Its banks are lined with other distinctive trees, notably *Acacia elatior*, a tall impressive tree with equally impressive thorns, and *Ficus sycamorus*, a wild fig whose fruits, borne in January and February, are much prized by monkeys and birds.

Mention must be made of the doum palm, *Hyphaene compressa*, the branching palm that marks the course of the river in its lower reaches. A coarse brew can be made from the palm sap, which perhaps gives rise to the story—almost certainly false—that elephants become drunk when they eat the fruit of the doum. By eating the fruit, however, they do distribute the seeds in a ready fertilized package. Another easily recognized tree, or more accurately a large shrub, is the toothbrush tree, *Salvadora persica*, whose abundance is due to the fact that most animals dislike it, although gerenuk will sometimes browse on it. Nevertheless, do not ignore this shrub as it is a favourite resting place of lion, and buffalo too. To the east of Samburu Lodge is a large salt pan covered with the salt bush, *Salsola Dendroides*, which again is not a greatly favoured food by many of the reserve's animals but which can be eaten in the absence of anything else. There are extensive areas of *Salsola* in Buffalo Springs, and some but not much in Shaba.

Much of all three reserves is covered by a plant community described by botanists as *Acacia commiphora* scrub. The classification of *commiphora* is a botanist's nightmare but the genus is easily recognized by the twisted branches and peeling, papery bark. It often hosts the parasite *Loranthus* whose pretty yellow or red flowers are easy to see, as the *commiphora* is so often without leaf. The trees yield a rich resin, one of them exuding myrrh, the incense of the Bible. The acacia genus is dominated in this area by *Acacia tortilis*, the 'umbrella tree'. The name comes from the twisted and contorted seed pods, which being rich in protein are relished by monkeys, impala, oryx, and even elephant, and which, outside the reserve, are the preferred food of goats. The umbrella tree flowers twice a year, just before the rains, and is then covered with a mass of creamy flowers, wonderful for bees and delightful to look at. The *Acacia commiphora* bushland is the favoured home of much of the wildlife, and it is here that you will find beisa oryx and Grevy's zebra (the two are often found together). Grant's gazelle and the reticulated giraffe are also inhabitants of the scrub, and if you are to see cheetah, this is the most likely habitat.

The riverine forest in the Samburu and Buffalo Springs reserves is much lusher than in Shaba. The denser, richer vegetation is favoured by waterbuck and impala, and although buffalo are still scarce (many died in the drought of 1984), their most likely locale is near the river.

During and for a short while after the rains, the reserves are alive with wild flowers. The desert rose, *Adenium obesum*, is perhaps the most distinctive. This succulent shrub, which sometimes grows to the size of a tree, bears copious pink to deep-rose flowers, giving way to long, thin, pinkish capsules about 20–25 centimetres (8–10 inches) long. These contain thin cylindrical seeds with tufts of fluffy white hairs at each end. When blown by the wind, these hairs act as wheels and send the spinning seed far from its parent. The henna plant, *Lawsonia inermis*, is a shrub or small tree that throws out a mass of small, creamy-white flowers on long, branching, spiny heads. This is the source of the dye that is widely used, in the east and on the coast, for colouring fingers and finger nails, the soles of the feet, and of course, as a hair conditioner and dye for textiles. But the most curious of the flowering plants in Samburu is undoubtedly *Caralluma russelliana*, which is large, erect, succulent, four-sided and without leaves, and sports a dense ball of deep purple, almost black flowers. Its earlier name, *C foetida*, reflected its rather nasty smell, which is alleged to attract flies for pollination.

Desert rose, Samburu

The best game-viewing is almost certainly along the river in the Samburu and Buffalo Springs reserves. Unfortunately, there is only one river crossing, so it is impossible to make a circuit using both sides of the river. The river edge in Shaba lacks the riparian forest, although doum palms proliferate, so game does not concentrate there in the same way as it does in the two westerly reserves. However, the views are special and there is a scenic backdrop of Mount Bodech.

Besides the river run you should also explore 'champagne ridge' in Buffalo Springs, where the shady acacias and lush grass attract many of the herbivores, including both common and Grevy's zebras. While in that area you can have a look at the springs themselves. Two have been walled and supply water to the nearby township of Archer's Post. You can swim in the walled pools, the walls having been built to save you from sharing the water with crocodiles. The latter are plentiful in the Uaso Ngiro River and there are numerous places where these reptiles can be seen. For a closer view, you can usually see the resident pair at the pool in front of Buffalo Springs Tented Lodge or you can visit the evening feeding ritual at Samburu Lodge. This display is not universally approved as some people regard the feeding of wild animals within a wildlife sanctuary as an ecological interference.

The central part of Samburu Reserve, around the mountain called Koitogorr, is a good area to see some of the dry zone species. The reticulated giraffe is, in fact, not a distinct species as it interbreeds with other races of giraffe, and you can see the results of such mixing in many parts of the country. You can certainly see it in zoos. But in Samburu the reticulated stands supreme as the other races seem unable to exist north of the equator. The world 'reticulated' refers to the netlike markings of the animal, the same Latin root providing the word 'reticulum' for the netlike sheath at the base of palm leaves. If the skin pattern is not enough by which to recognize a reticulated giraffe, a second obvious characteristic is the conspicuous central horn between the eyes. The giraffe's gait is similar to that of the camel, whereby both legs on one side move forward together, a movement known as 'pacing'. The only other animal to move in this way when walking is the brown bear.

Samburu—arid, harsh and savagely beautiful

Grevy's zebra are also only found north of the equator. The sparse feed results in small herds and the Grevy is rarely seen in groups of more than a dozen, although in Buffalo Springs and in richer grasslands to the south it mixes with the common zebra (but does not interbreed). The Grevy is named after the French President Grevy, who received one of the animals as a gift from the Negus, or King of Shewa, in southern Ethiopia in 1881.

Beisa oryx are also only found north of the equator, and thus the three Samburu reserves are the only protected areas where these beautiful animals can be found in Kenya. The beisa's near relative, the fringe-eared oryx, can be seen in Amboseli and in Tsavo. It is very similar to the beisa but is more rufous and, of course, has distinct fringes to its ears. Both sexes carry rapier-like horns that present an awesome aspect to a menacing predator. Oryx are among the few antelopes that resist attack from lions. The side view of an oryx—when it may seem to have only one horn—is said to have given rise to the origin of the legendary unicorn. Beisa move in herds of up to 50 animals, mainly cows and calves, with the bulls often leading a solitary life. When an oryx takes flight, notice how the chin is thrust up and the head moves from side to side in rhythm with the pace of the forelegs.

Also to be seen in Samburu is the northern, or Somali race of ostrich, whose thighs and neck are blue rather than the flesh-pink of the Masai ostrich. The ostrich is the world's largest bird, standing from two to two and a half metres (seven to eight feet) high. A cock ostrich may stay with several hens, all of which lay their eggs in the same nest. During the day the hens sit on the nest, while the much more conspicuous male takes his turn at night. Up to 40 eggs have been found in one nest, and 30 are quite common.

The gerenuk is another unmistakable animal. Coloured much like an impala, its long neck gives it its Swahili name *swala twiga*—the giraffe antelope. The word *gerenuk* is Somali in origin and also refers to its distinctive elongated neck. This antelope is found in eastern and northeastern Kenya and well into southern Ethiopia and Somalia. In fact, it has the widest range of any of the East African gazelles. Gerunuk neither drink nor graze, deriving their total nourishment from browsing the leaves of hostile acacia trees and shrubs. The gerenuk is among the most graceful of creatures when it stands erect on its hind legs in order to reach the higher branches, yet when it walks it seems as though its head is too heavy and it slouches with drooping shoulders and hunched body. No doubt this is an adaptation for passing through thornbush and prickly scrub like a duiker. Only the males have horns.

You can see both Kirk's and Guenther's dikdik throughout Samburu, but Kirk's is more common. Guenther's is slightly bigger and generally has an overall greyer colour but it is best distinguished by its more elongated, almost trunk-like nose. Guenther's is found only in northern Kenya and Somalia but Kirk's is found as far south as Namibia. Both sexes have horns and both races are rarely found in groups of more than two or three.

The western part of Samburu is hillier and the tracks rougher than in the central area but it is worth a visit if only for the solitude and the spectacular views. Mount Kenya can be seen from the elevated parts of all three reserves. It is also possible to exit and enter the Samburu National Reserve via the West Gate, but a four-wheel-drive vehicle is recommended for this route. There are several sand *luggas* or dry watercourses (except when it rains, when they become torrents) on the road to the West Gate. Although these can be negotiated by minibuses and other two-wheel-drive cars, a crossing should only be attempted when the sand is dry.

Birdlife in the three reserves is, as almost everywhere in Kenya, prolific. Over 400 species have been recorded, many of them birds that you will not see elsewhere on your safari. After the ostrich, the next most distinctive birds will be the hornbills. Four species occur: the yellow-billed, the red-billed, Von der Decken's and the grey hornbill. The hornbill family has remarkable breeding habits, with the female being imprisoned in her nesting hole in a tree by the male, who plasters up the entrance and feeds her through a small slit during the whole of the incubation period. You may well be able to observe this performance within the grounds of your lodge or camp.

The kori bustard is another large bird, found on the open plains. Its sedate walk while it searches for food (mice, grasshoppers, small snakes, and fruits—the same diet as the hornbills) and its height make this bird unmistakable. If you are very lucky you may see the mating display in which the male appears to stand on tip-toe, inflating his neck so that the head is lost apart from the skyward pointing bill. At the same time, he manages to lift his tail vertically and even bend it forwards over his back. The white, black-bellied and the smaller buff-crested bustards are also resident at Samburu. Of the game-birds, the yellow-necked spurfowl is everywhere, as too is the handsome and gregarious vulturine guinea fowl, who sports electric-blue breast feathers.

Twenty-four birds of prey are resident within the three reserves. The bateleur is frequently seen, usually on the wing and easily distinguished by its minute tail, or apparent absence of a tail. Also frequently seen is the tiny pygmy falcon; the male has a grey back while the female is rufous brown. The next most common bird of prey, excluding the vultures, is the pale chanting goshawk, unmistakable because of its upright stance and long, orange-red legs.

This is not the place to describe the long list of birds found in Samburu, but it should be quite possible to identify at least 50 species while taking a two- to three-hour game drive. In a two-day stay at Samburu, even if you are not on a specifically bird-watching safari, you should be able to list 100 species. Of course, you will be greatly helped by having a knowledgeable driver-guide. In any event, no visitor

should start his or her safari without a copy of John Williams's *Field Guide to the Birds of East Africa* (see Recommended Reading, pp 202–3). If you can, try to obtain a checklist that will also help in eliminating bad or poor identification. One such list is included in the small guidebook to the three Samburu reserves published by the Friends of Conservation.

ACCOMMODATION

■ LODGES IN THE RESERVES
Samburu Lodge (141 beds, 4 stars) in Samburu N R
Samburu Serena Lodge (88 beds, 4 stars) in Buffalo Springs N R
Sarova Shaba Lodge (170 beds, unclassified) in Shaba N R

■ TENTED LODGES
Samburu Intrepids Club (50 beds, unclassified) in Samburu N R
Buffalo Springs Lodge (77 beds, 3 stars) in Buffalo Springs N R

■ TENTED CAMPS
Larsen's (34 beds, unclassified) in Samburu N R

Reticulated giraffe, Samburu: netlike markings and a central horn

Amboseli National Park

Amboseli is an astonishing place. It is like a three-dimensional tapestry where there is so much activity that it is hard to know where to look and easier still to overlook something. The majestic backdrop of Africa's highest mountain, Kilimanjaro, presides over a tranquil landscape, a vast plain that is dry, dusty and white, except where the waters from the forests of Kilimanjaro emerge as swamps and carve out lush, verdant retreats for elephant and hippo. This is a landscape that is still evolving, where water suddenly appears almost overnight and trees die, sometimes of drought, sometimes of drowning. Soil becomes more saline and the fever trees yield to salt bush. Encouraged by underground water, the wild date palm, *Phoenix reclinata*, by nature gregarious, is creating barriers to everyone and everything, except perhaps the elephants. This everchanging environment contrasts with the stability of the parks and reserves, where the ecosystem has 'climaxed' and the landscape become changeless. In the Mara, it seems as though the landscape has not changed since the world began. In Amboseli, one feels the movement of time, the vibrations of change. Perhaps it is because one can always see movement—of wild animals in their endless search for food; of the Masai who roam with their cattle through Amboseli in their interminable quest for water; of vehicles issuing twice-daily from the lodges to view the miracle that is Amboseli, carrying occupants largely unaware of their part in an unfolding evolutionary drama. Each of the four components—the wildlife, the Masai, the visitors, and the climate—makes its own contribution, large or small, to the scene.

There are three routes to Amboseli. If you are starting from Nairobi you will probably take the tarmac road for about 160 kilometres (110 miles) to Namanga on the Tanzanian border, and then turn east along a heavily corrugated track for another 80 kilometres (50 miles) to the park. Your driver may choose to turn off this diabolical route soon after leaving the tarmac road, but that will mean you are taking the Oloitiptip road (named after a distinguished post-independence Masai leader), which is smoother but a good deal dustier. It is actually a little longer that way but perhaps a little quicker. From either of these routes you arrive near Lake Amboseli, which for most of the year is a dry bed of grey soda. If the annual 'long rains' are heavy, water stays on the lake bed for a few months but is never more than 60 centimetres (two feet) in depth.

Surprisingly, wildebeest are often seen scattered over the dry lake bed, where not a sign of vegetation exists and where the heat of the day is most trying. Zebra and even giraffe may also be seen on this featureless expanse but they are crossing it, unlike the wildebeest, which seem to enjoy isolation. Despite their highly developed social system, male wildebeest are often solitary; as many as one in seven move away from the herd, except when nature calls in March and the rutting begins. Although the Amboseli wildebeest are always on the move, they do not migrate in the way that their kin do in the Serengeti. The most likely reason is that they are now too confined to do so, but the instinct is there and in the park they can be seen trekking in long lines, perhaps to where some grazing may exist after a recent rainstorm. Not only are they confined by human encroachment but also by the need for water, for they drink almost daily and so cannot range far from permanent water.

The fringe-eared oryx, on the other hand, which is found also in Amboseli, is quite likely not to drink at all during the whole of its lifetime. While the wildebeest can live in this semi-desert because of the swamps, the oryx disdains the water. Its secret is that it feeds mostly at night. During the night the grass and herbs that survive in near-desert conditions do so by taking up moisture produced by condensation, since the humidity rises as the temperature falls. If this relatively succulent meal is eaten at night, before the heat of the day desiccates it once again, the oryx gets sufficient water. It has been estimated that in the course of one night's feeding an oryx ingests the four litres (one gallon) of water that its 180 kilograms (400 pounds) of body weight requires.

The other main route to Amboseli also starts from Nairobi, but follows the Mombasa road as far as Emali, along 130 kilometres (80 miles) of tarmac. Then a right turn leads almost due south, heading for the border town of Loitokitok. The road to the park's Lemboti Gate is found on the right after about 55 kilometres (35 miles), and the road to the Kimana Gate a further 30 kilometres (18 miles) towards Loitokitok. This will be the road you are taking if you come from Tsavo Park direct, or if you are staying at Kilimanjaro Buffalo Lodge.

Amboseli has been a national park only since 1977, and its birth pangs were painful. In 1906, the colonial government created the 'Southern Masai Game Reserve', a huge area that not only included Amboseli but all the land between it and the Masai Mara. The idea at that time was to give some protection to the elephant during the time of the ivory trade, a grotesque period when trading in slaves gave way to trading in ivory. Both Tsavo and Nairobi National Parks were gazetted in the 1940s, but Amboseli could not be brought into this new network because of its human population. In 1948, it was designated a reserve, acknowledging the rights of the Masai to stay where they were. The new reserve, of 3,260 square kilometres (1,260 square miles), was all that remained of the vast tract that had been set aside in 1906. But the strident pleas of conservationists, who believed that over-use by the Masai was destroying the reserve, were heard in government circles. In 1970, President Kenyatta was persuaded to set apart a sanctuary area of 389 square kilometres (150 square miles) in the area around the main swamps. The Masai retaliated by killing almost all

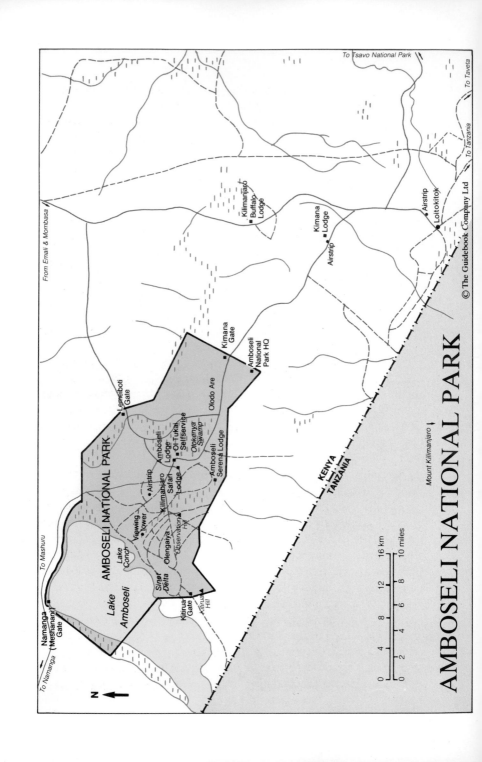

AMBOSELI NATIONAL PARK

© The Guidebook Company Ltd

the rhino for which the reserve was especially famous. To underline their feelings, they left behind the much-prized horns with the carcasses.

The eternal argument about water for the Masai cattle dragged on as it had done for the previous 25 years. Finally, some of the swamp area was exchanged for some dry land in the north, and the boundaries of the new national park were agreed. These were gazetted in 1977. But the difficulties were not over. Whenever there is a drought, which seems to be most of the time, the park is invaded by cattle and their owners, ostensibly for water but also for grazing. Until there is sufficient money to pipe water out of the park—and to keep the water flowing—the warden will be unable to do anything about the daily invasion.

The Masai live in harmony with the wildlife, and damage is therefore restricted to the terrain, where thousands of cattle hooves are destroying the fragile vegetation. It would seem, however, that much more damage is being done to the park by the wild animals themselves. When Joseph Thomson (whose name is perpetuated by Thomson's gazelle) visited the Amboseli area in 1883, he failed to mention the presence of elephant, although he described graphically the quantity and the variety of the game. 'In spite of the desolate and barren aspect of the country,' he wrote, 'game is to be seen in marvellous abundance. The giraffe, fit denizen of such a region, appears against the horizon like some unearthly monster, or browses among the trees and bushes. The wildebeest, imp-like and fierce in appearance, frisks with uncouth movements, or speeds with stiff, ungainly gallops across the natron plain. Zebras in long lines pace leisurely along from some distant pasture-ground. Hyenas slink home from their meal of carrion. Lions, satisfied with the night's venture, express their sense of repletion with reverberating roars.'

Everything but elephants in this 'marvellous abundance'. There are now over 700 elephants in the Amboseli National Park. The land over which elephants roamed in Thomson's day was vast, and human pressure almost totally non-existent; today, elephants are almost entirely confined to the park and the damage they inflict on their present habitat is there for all to see. Most observers believe that elephants destroy trees only when outside influences make that a necessity. It is certainly true that as farming developed on the fringes of the park, more and more trees were pushed over or de-barked within the sanctuary. So much of the devastation of trees that can be seen by visitors today is elephant damage, and only some the result of salt coming nearer the surface with the rising water table. It would seem that the yellow-barked acacias (fever trees) are particularly vulnerable to the salt problem. Damage to other species of acacia is almost certainly caused by elephants.

Without water the park simply would not exist, so one has to accept the disadvantages of the rising water table and the consequent destruction of the fever trees.

Similarly, without the co-operation of the Masai there would not be a park, so the destruction by their cattle also has to be accepted. Then there is the problem of the tourists and their vehicles. Some of the money that the park earns from entry fees goes to the local people, giving the less altruistic a more tangible reason to maintain the park. So the tourists have to be accepted as well, despite the destruction caused by their wheels.

These are some of the paradoxes that the wildlife authorities have to address if Amboseli is to survive as one of the world's great animal refuges. And now a master plan, which has taken years to evolve, has at last emerged. Not much of the foregoing need concern the average visitor and is related here only by way of answering the question that most visitors ask: why does this park have such a forlorn, yet vibrant feel to it?

As may already be clear, elephants are the most conspicuous of Amboseli's wild-life. The park provides an ideal location for elephant research. Cynthia Moss, whose books about the Amboseli elephants have become world-famous, has carried out long-term research in the park. Katharine Payne, who pioneered research into elephant communication by 'infrasound', has also done research in Amboseli. Infrasound is almost certainly the means by which a female elephant makes it known to distant males that she is in oestrus. Joyce Poole, whose doctoral research on the lives of male elephants was also carried out in Amboseli, speculated on how a female, who comes into oestrus for just a few days every four or five years, could be immediately surrounded by males as soon as the condition arose. Many of these males had travelled for many miles to attend. A major question yet to be answered by the researchers—or indeed by anyone else—is what will happen to the park as elephant numbers continue to increase? Or put the other way round: what will happen to the elephants when the park can no longer accommodate them? The short answer is that no one knows. Studies continue and scientists disagree.

Generally there are nursery herds of female elephants and their young, as well as groups of bulls of all ages gathered into 'bachelor herds'. A female breeds once every four or perhaps five years, and a 'family' consists of perhaps six members: the senior female, her daughters and her granddaughters, and maybe a male calf not yet mature enough to have left the herd. Families stay together in the family herd and may do so for long periods of time—40 years is not unusual. The social cohesion of the bachelor herds is far looser, with bulls seeming to come and go as they see fit. Sometimes the bachelor herds appear to be territorial, but not always.

It is the intimacy of the family structure that endears this massive beast to humans. A scream from a calf brings the whole herd to its aid, and rarely do elephants show any sign of having differences with their relatives or companions. They travel,

Mother elephants are intensely protective of their young

eat, drink, and sleep in enviable cooperation, evoking admiration and jealousy from their human observers who are not capable of anything like such peaceful coexistence. Eating takes place all day and all night, and their food intake is about 45 kilograms (100 pounds) per tonne weight. A fully grown animal will therefore consume around 315 kilograms (700 pounds) a day—and much more when vegetation is readily available. Taking the calculation further, one elephant will eat about 4,000 tonnes of food in its lifetime. However, their digestion is not all that efficient, with less than 50 per cent of what is eaten being digested. Their droppings average nearly eight kilograms (17 pounds) and, in order to release some 135 kilograms (300 pounds) of waste, about 17 deposits a day need to be made. This enormous transfer of vegetation amounts, in Amboseli alone, to over 100,000 kilograms per day, or 36,500 tonnes a year. In addition to depositing huge amounts of fertilizer, the elephant's feet trample vegetation, which acts both as a fertilizer and a shade from the scorching sun. All of this adds up to a richer, and more active soil. But these things are only in balance where there is unlimited space and no interruption or interference by man. And that is not the case in Amboseli.

The life expectancy of an elephant has more to do with its teeth than any other factor. Although the tusks are strictly speaking teeth (upside down outside, according to Ogden Nash), the elephant has only four cheek teeth, which in a grown adult are up to 30 centimetres (one foot) long. As the teeth are worn down by the incessant grinding of food they are replaced six times. After the last set are worn out, the end cannot be far away.

Your first drive in Amboseli will almost certainly involve a circuit of the swamp area. Some of the older elephants live permanently in the swamps, savouring the soft reeds and ignoring the drier vegetation that their worn-out teeth cannot grind. But hippo also live in the swamps, particularly the larger expanses of water to the west. In Amboseli, hippos are not normally seen out of the water in daytime, so the most you are likely to see is some frolicking in the water, or their four-toed footprints on the fringes of the swamp. There are not very many hippos in the area, as they much prefer grass to the swamp reeds and other aquatic vegetation. Since there is so little grass in the vicinity (and a hippo eats about 70 kilograms [150 pounds] of grass each night), some form of natural birth control is taking place. In ideal conditions a hippo will produce a calf every three years, from the age of ten onwards, so in a lifespan of 40 years a hippo mother will normally produce ten calves. The calves are born under water and are suckled there, milk being pumped by the mother in the same way that whales feed their young. Soon the calf learns to travel by riding on its mother's back. Hippo and crocodile get along quite well, but crocodile are not present at Amboseli.

Leopard, cheetah, rhino and buffalo are all found in Amboseli and your visit to the park will be better rewarded if you pursue your quarry well off the beaten track. That does not mean off the established tracks and roads, but quartering the less frequented parts of the park. Currently (in 1991) there is only one pair of lion in the whole park. An early walk up Observation Hill not only offers superb views but may also let you get sight of, and a bearing on some of the less obvious inhabitants. In any case, it offers a little exercise, something that you will find is sadly lacking in the average Kenya safari. Another walk has been recently opened at Kitirua. You will need a ranger as an escort, but this is easily arranged at the nearby Kitirua Ranger Post. Make sure you carry something to drink, and wear a hat, and you will find this an exciting diversion from the daily routine of game drives.

Three antelope are found in the bush areas surrounding the park. The lesser kudu, best seen in the early morning or late afternoon, is primarily a browser, eating leaves, seed pods and fruit, although it does graze too, unlike its larger relative, the greater kudu (which is not found in Amboseli). The lesser kudu also eats *Sansevieria* —'mother-in-law's tongue'—one of the few animals known to do so. Found in small herds of up to six, lesser kudu are naturally shy and the most you may see of them is their striped, sleek grey bodies moving off in a characteristic rocking-horse motion. Only the males carry the elegant spiralled horns. In much the same habitat you may also come across the gerenuk, greyer here than in Samburu, and the fringe-eared oryx. These are found in small herds of up to 30, but once again they are shy and tend to take flight as you stop the car for photography.

A word about the birds of Amboseli. The most obvious is the superb starling, who will happily share your breakfast table with you given the slightest chance, and almost certainly, not far away, will be his look-alike, Hildebrandt's starling, with much the same colouring but without the white breast band. The marshes and swamps attract a great number of water birds. A wonderful sight (and sound) is the arrival of hundreds of sandgrouse at their favourite waterhole, announcing the fact with a cacophony of guttural clicks.

There are always a few flamingo to be seen but with the recent arrival of more standing water there are now quite considerable numbers. As is usual where flamingo are found, so too are pelicans. Both the white pelican and the pink-backed are visitors when water conditions are right. Eleven herons are resident, among them the magnificent goliath heron and the faithful cattle egret, searching for insects in the wake of his giant companion. Birds of prey are evident everywhere and Williams claims in his *Field Guide* that 17 different kinds have been recorded in or near the park.

ACCOMMODATION

■ LODGES IN THE PARK
Amboseli Serena Lodge (76 rooms, 5 stars)
Amboseli Lodge (224 beds, 3 stars)
Kilimanjaro Safari Lodge (204 beds, 2 stars)
Ol Tukai Self-help cottages are in the park near Amboseli Lodge.

■ LODGES OUTSIDE THE PARK
Kilimanjaro Buffalo Lodge (200 beds, 4 stars)
Kimana Lodge (48 beds, 1 star)
There is a camp site just outside the park perimeter.

Hippos (left); *rock python* (above)

Tsavo National Park

This is Kenya's largest national park, divided into two—Tsavo East and Tsavo West. It occupies 20,872 square kilometres (8,050 square miles), roughly the size of Wales or Israel. Tsavo East and Tsavo West are separated by the main Nairobi–Mombasa Road. Tsavo East is the larger section, about 11,000 square kilometres (4,250 square miles), but is drier and less frequented than Tsavo West. A large part of Tsavo East is also closed to the public, partly because of its inaccessibility and partly as a refuge for wildlife. There are only two permanent rivers in Tsavo, one being the river after which the park is named and the other the Athi, which begins its journey to the sea not far from Nairobi. Where the Tsavo and Athi rivers meet, just above Lugard's Falls, the river becomes the Galana and enters the Indian Ocean just north of Malindi. The rest of the park is not exactly waterless, since there are many man-made waterholes. The Voi River, which dries up periodically, feeds a large man-made reservoir of 85 hectares (210 acres) at Aruba, arguably the best place in Tsavo East for game. Most of the park consists of basement schists, except for the northern part of Tsavo West, where recent volcanic activity has transformed the landscape. The road to Tsavo from Amboseli passes over a recent lava flow and beside the perfect cone of a new volcano called Shitani or *Shaitani* (which is Swahili for 'Devil'). Here you can also see the volcanic range known as the Chyulu Hills and its attendant cones, all 600 of them, in an almost lunar landscape. This is an area of Tsavo that must be seen, despite the road.

Tsavo West is by far the more attractive of the two Tsavos and if time permits visiting only one section, Go West. There is a great diversity of terrain: open plains, bush that is sometimes almost impenetrable, acacia woodlands, hills and huge rocky outcrops, thick riverine forest— in fact, drama everywhere. In addition, there are over 60 species of mammal, 500 bird species, and plants and trees both beautiful and grotesque. The baobab tree fits both these categories and makes Tsavo different from every other major park in Kenya. The plains are everywhere littered with baobabs, which are reputed to survive up to 300 years, if the elephants leave them alone. That in itself is a problem, since elephants relish the bark, which contains plenty of calcium (although stripping the bark does not kill the tree), and in times of drought, they tusk into the interior to obtain liquid. It is rare to see a young baobab, since elephants find the whole young tree especially palatable. A national park ought to protect its trees as well as its fauna, but no warden has yet found a way of protecting the baobab. The pulp that surrounds the seeds within the large, 22-centimetre (9-inch) capsule is not only edible but refreshing and contains large amounts of vitamin C. When the tree flowers after rain it produces a number of pretty, waxy white petals surrounding a ball of fine stamens. Unfortunately, the scent is quite unpleasant, though clearly attractive to the flies that pollinate the tree.

The desert rose is also found in Tsavo. This strange plant, which looks a little like a miniature baobab, becomes covered with deep pink flowers at the height of the dry season. The acacia family is also well represented, with the familiar *Acacia tortilis* present throughout the plains and *Acacia xcanthophloea* along the banks of the permanent rivers. Look out for some of the smaller but interesting plants like *Adenia globosa*, which presents a tangled mass of green spiky branches but no leaves, emerging from a huge, rock-like root above the soil.

One of the first places you may visit in Tsavo West is Mzima Springs. The springs support a true oasis surrounding two pools—the long pool and the top pool—the former home to numerous hippos who live and breed there. The crystal water that emerges after its journey from the Chyulu Hills 40–50 kilometres (25–30 miles) away, flows at a rate of 225 million litres (50 million gallons) per day. This is the source of Mombasa's water supply, but the intake is well hidden and you will not be aware of the presence of this alien intrusion. Because the water is so clear the hippos can be seen walking on the floor of the pool like marionettes, their huge bulk supported by the water's invisible buoyancy. Four types of fish swim around them but the larger shoals are barbel. From a small wooden tower you can survey the scene and maybe spot a crocodile, for there are plenty of them at Mzima. There is an underwater glass-sided tank, where the hippos' underwater ballet can be observed with some awe. The pools are surrounded by wild date palms and raphia palms; their magnificent foliage, which yields raffia and a wax, have made them candidates for extinction in Kenya. You will also see the doum palm. This is the same tree that is found in riparian situations in Samburu. When leaving the long pool, the water flows underground for a few metres to emerge as the Mzima River, which joins the Tsavo River seven kilometres (four miles) downstream.

Having located Mzima, you are in the nerve centre of Tsavo West and roughly half-way between the two wildlife lodges, Kilaguni and Ngulia. The former has a waterhole that seems to be in constant use day and night, and the lodge grounds are inhabited by all sorts of small creatures, such as ground squirrels and mongooses, and even bigger creatures like warthog. Birds, too, are extremely friendly. The hornbills and the inevitable superb starlings offer serious competition to human discourse. This is also a good place to study the agama lizard, very common throughout Kenya; the orange and blue colouring of the male is quite unmistakable. It is an extremely agile creature, leaping from rock to rock and climbing vertical faces with complete confidence. It feeds on insects, small frogs, and sometimes its own young.

The verandah of Kilaguni may also be a suitable place to think about termites. On your journey through Tsavo you will have seen plenty of termite mounds; indeed,

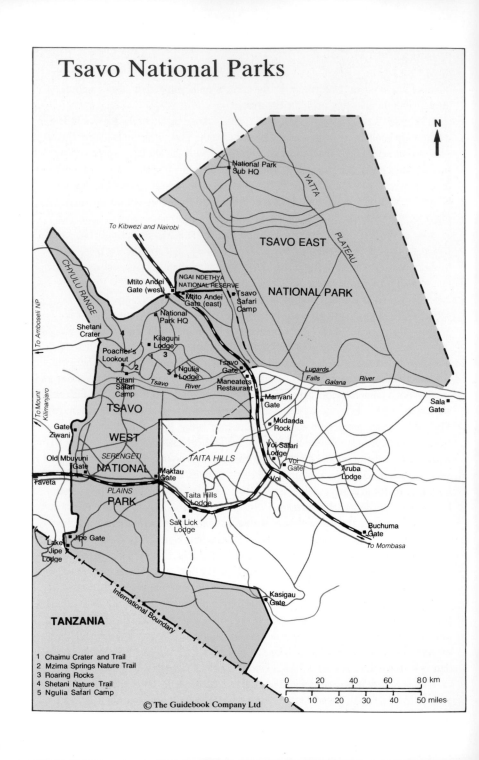

Tsavo National Parks

N

To Kibwezi and Nairobi

CHYULU RANGE

To Amboseli NP

TSAVO EAST

National Park Sub HQ

YATTA PLATEAU

NATIONAL PARK

Mtito Andei Gate (west)

NGAI NDETHYA NATIONAL RESERVE

Mtito Andei Gate (east)

Tsavo Safari Camp

Shetani Crater

National Park HQ

4

Kilaguni Lodge

3

Poacher's Lookout

2

1

Ngulia Lodge

5

Tsavo Gate

Maneaters Restaurant

Lugards Falls

Galana River

To Mount Kilimanjaro

Kitani Safari Camp

Tsavo River

Manyani Gate

Sala Gate

Gate Ziwani

TSAVO

Mudanda Rock

WEST

Voi Safari Lodge

Old Mbuyuni Gate

SERENGETI

NATIONAL

TAITA HILLS

Voi Gate

Aruba Lodge

Taveta

Maktau Gate

Voi

PLAINS

PARK

Taita Hills Lodge

Salt Lick Lodge

Buchuma Gate

To Mombasa

Lake Jipe Lodge

Jipe Gate

Kasigau Gate

International Boundary

TANZANIA

1 Chaimu Crater and Trail
2 Mzima Springs Nature Trail
3 Roaring Rocks
4 Shetani Nature Trail
5 Ngulia Safari Camp

0   20   40   60   80 km

0   10   20   30   40   50 miles

© The Guidebook Company Ltd

Termite mound near Namanga: Kenya is home to about 400 species

these can be found in one shape or another in almost any part of Kenya, which is home to about 400 species. Termites have not changed their form in a hundred million years and there are more of them than any other living creature. Termites live off decaying wood or other vegetable or even animal material, which they reach by tunnelling from their nest. On returning to the nest the workers regurgitate this food (or excrete it), and it is eaten a second time by residents who may feel hungry. Having been ingested perhaps several times, only a brown paste remains and that is used to bind the soil into the hard-as-iron castles that form the termites' homes.

Elephants are making a comeback after years of attrition by drought and poachers. Not that long ago, half of all the elephants in Kenya were concentrated in Tsavo. There may have been as many as 23,000. The experts differed on the numbers, but it was generally agreed that there were too many for the park to sustain. Some favoured letting nature take its course; others favoured a cull. But then you can't just send in an army of sharpshooters and annihilate those elephants who happen to be in the way. There must be a better policy. While the issue was being discussed, however, drought took over and by the end of 1971 at least 3,000 elephants had died. Then came organized, mechanized poaching. Gangs armed with automatic weapons devastated the elephant herds. And the rhino suffered as well. David Sheldrick, then Warden of Tsavo, estimated that as many as 1,300 poachers were at work in Tsavo at the same time. The government fought back, but fighting poachers is like a guerrilla war, in which the advantage is always with the enemy.

By the mid-1980s, and with only 3,000 elephants left in the Tsavo ecosystem, poaching was finally contained. Now the situation has improved still further and as long as the current vigilance is maintained, there is no threat to the elephants of Tsavo. The international ban on ivory trading has helped dramatically as the market has almost vanished. If the ban is continued, as Kenya hopes, then the elephant has a future. It is still a far cry, however, from the vast herds that strolled through the country only a century ago. One of the results of the over-population of elephants in the 1960s was the destruction of much of the bushland and the creation of open grasslands. There are now visible signs of a return of the bush that was once eaten or trampled out of existence.

The rhino, not only in Tsavo but in all Kenya, came close to extinction. In 1960, there were estimated to be over 20,000 rhino in Kenya. By 1985, that population had been reduced to 450. Tsavo once held one of the last great concentrations of rhinos on earth. These suffered dramatically in the droughts of the 1970s—600 were estimated to have died at that time—and the poachers nearly finished off the remainder. The good news is that there is now a rhino sanctuary near Ngulia, and slowly but surely the rhino population will be rebuilt.

Not far from Mzima Springs are the Roaring Rocks. No one knows how they got this name, though they are said to whistle in a high wind. There is an interesting observation post on the top, and the short walk will be welcomed. From the top you should be able to plan your next move as game concentrations can be observed over great distances. The route to Ngulia via Rhino Valley is usually rewarding (but not with rhino), and the backdrop of the Ngulia range quite staggering. Do not miss the Chaimu lava flow, where there are indications of blow holes, lava fountains, sulphur deposits and other reminders of the vast forces that were unleashed only a few hundred years ago in what must have been a spectacular demonstration of nature's power.

There are several places in Tsavo East that deserve special mention. Mudanda Rock, a miniature version of Australia's Ayers Rock, is not only impressive in its own right (it is nearly two kilometres, or one mile, long) but in dry weather a climb to the summit—less arduous than it sounds—reveals a water hole at its eastern foot, often attended by large herds of elephant and buffalo. The drive starting at Voi Lodge continues to join the Athi River and a pretty route following the watercourse allows you to spot crocodile until you reach Lugard's Falls. These are more of a curiosity than a spectacle, since the waters of the Athi plunge through a fissure scarcely more than a metre wide. Quite an easy leap will take you across—unless you happen to have noticed the signboard to Crocodile Point just below. You may decide not to jump. In any case, the park on the other bank is technically 'closed to the public'.

From Lugard's Falls you should head east along the river to Sobo and thence south to Aruba Dam, a large 85-hectare (210-acre) man-made lake, where many animals water and birdlife is often spectacular. If you intend to leave the park for Malindi, you should miss out Aruba and drive along the river to the Sala Gate, with only 110 kilometers (69 miles) to go on a dry-weather road before you reach the Indian Ocean.

From Aruba you can leave the park via the Buchuma Gate if you are heading for Mombasa, or through the Voi Gate if you are heading for Nairobi or the Taita Hills. The Taita Hills Sanctuary is a privately owned, 11,500-hectare (28,000-acre) game ranch that is well stocked with lion and elephant and served by two elegant game lodges. Tsavo West is easily entered from the Taita Hills Sanctuary via the Maktau Gate, and access is also simple to Lake Jipe, a marshy but delightful stretch of water that straddles the Kenya–Tanzania border. Boats can be hired and bird-and-hippo watching is more than satisfactory. You may see the fringe-eared oryx on the way to or from Jipe.

ACCOMMODATION

■ IN TSAVO WEST (OR NEAR)
Kilaguni Lodge (104 beds,4 stars)
Ngulia Lodge (104 beds, 4 stars)
Lake Jipe Lodge (50 beds, stars)

SELF-HELP CAMPS
Ngulia and Kitani. There is a new 16-bed tented camp at Ziwani, on the Lumi River, just outside the western boundary of Tsavo West.

■ IN TSAVO EAST (OR NEAR)
Voi Safari Lodge (100 beds, 4 stars)

TENTED CAMPS
Tsavo Safari Camp (40 beds, 2 stars)
Crocodile Camp (40 beds, 1 star)
Aruba Self-help lodge

■ IN TAITA HILLS SANCTUARY
Taita Hills Lodge (124 beds, 5 stars)
Salt Lick lodge (128 beds, 4 stars), a night observation lodge built on stilts.

(following pages) *Lake Magadi*

To The Interior

In the early morning we start from Mombasa Station, taking our places upon an ordinary garden seat fastened on to the cow-catcher of the engine, from which position the whole country can be seen. For a quarter of an hour we are still upon Mombasa Island, and then the train, crossing the intervening channel by a long iron bridge, addresses itself in earnest to the continent of Africa. Into these vast regions the line winds perseveringly upon a stiff up-grade, and the land unfolds itself ridge after ridge and valley after valley, till soon, with one farewell glance at the sea and at the fighting-tops of His Majesty's ship Venus rising queerly amid the palms, we are embraced and engulfed completely. All day long the train runs upward and westward, through broken and undulating ground clad and encumbered with super-abundant vegetation. Beautiful birds and butterflies fly from tree to tree and flower to flower. Deep, ragged gorges, filled by streams in flood, open out far below us through glades of palms and creeper-covered trees. Here and there, at intervals, which will become shorter every year, are plantations of rubber, fibre, and cotton, the beginnings of those inexhaustible supplies which will one day meet the yet unmeasured demand of Europe for those indispensable commodities. Every few miles are little trim stations, with their water-tanks, signals, ticket-offices, and flower-beds complete and all of a pattern, backed by impenetrable bush. In brief one slender thread of scientific civilization, of order, authority, and arrangement, drawn across the primeval chaos of the world.

In the evening a cooler, crisper air is blowing. The humid coast lands, with their glories and their fevers, have been left behind. At an altitude of four thousand feet we begin to laugh at the Equator. The jungle becomes forest, not less luxuriant, but distinctly different in character. The olive replaces the palm. The whole aspect of the land is more friendly, more familiar, and no less fertile. After Makindu Station the forest ceases. The traveller enters upon a region of grass. Immense fields of green pasture, withered and whitened at this season by waiting for the rains, intersected by streams and watercourses densely wooded with dark, fir-looking trees and gorse-looking scrub, and relieved by bold upstanding bluffs and ridges, comprise the new panorama. And here is presented the wonderful and unique spectacle which the Uganda Railway offers to the European. The plains are crowded with wild animals. From the windows of the carriage the whole zoological gardens can be seen disporting itself. Herds of antelope and gazelle, troops of zebras—sometimes four or five hundred together—watch the train pass with placid assurance, or scamper a hundred yards further away, and turn again. Many are quite close to the line. With field-glasses one can see that it is the same everywhere, and can distinguish long files of black wildebeeste and herds of red kongoni—the hartebeeste of South Africa—and wild ostriches walking sedately in twos and threes, and every kind of small deer and gazelle. The zebras come close enough for their stripes to be admired with the naked eye.

We have arrived at Simba, 'The Place of Lions', and there is no reason why the passengers should not see one, or even half-a-dozen, stalking across the plain, respectfully observed by lesser beasts. Indeed, in the early days it was the custom to stop and sally out upon the royal vermin whenever met with, and many the lion that has been carried back to the tender in triumph before the guard, or driver, or anyone else could think of time-tables or the block system, or the other inconvenient restrictions of a regular service. Farther up the line, in the twilight of the evening, we saw, not a hundred yards away, a dozen giraffes lolloping off among scattered trees, and at Nakuru six yellow lions walked in leisurely mood across the rails in broad daylight. Only the rhinoceros is absent, or rarely seen, and after one of his species had measured his strength, unsuccessfully, against an engine, he has confined himself morosely to the river-beds and to the undisturbed solitudes which, at a distance of two or three miles, everywhere engulf the Uganda Railway.

Winston Churchill, My African Journey, *1908*

Meru National Park

Meru is the least known of Kenya's major parks, despite the fame generated by Elsa, Joy Adamson's celebrated lioness who returned to the wild here. It deserves to be known better, since it is not only a wildlife stronghold but the park with the most diverse scenery. Its southern boundary is the Tana River, at an altitude of 365 metres (1,000 feet), and in the north the foothills of the Nyambene Mountains at roughly three times that height. Within the park are 15 permanent rivers, mostly quite small but large enough to harbour crocodiles. The prettiest of the rivers, the Rojewero, bisects the park west to east and provides delightful riverine scenery as well as a midday refuge for much wildlife. The park has had its share of poaching but happily that is no longer the case. The herds are being rebuilt and game viewing should be splendid. Some of the biggest elephant herds in the country can now be found in this park. Buffalo, too, are plentiful and are often in large numbers. If you are not going farther north to Samburu, you will have the chance in Meru to see some of the typical northern species, especially the reticulated giraffe and Grevy's zebra. The common zebra is also found in the park. Among the less common animals you will also find the beisa oryx, lesser kudu and the gerenuk. All the large cats are represented, and leopards are now being seen quite frequently.

A visit to the Tana River will take up the best part of a day. It can be extremely hot in the south of the park, so an expedition to the Tana should be taken quite seriously. Plenty of water and sun protection are absolutely essential. Game is scarce in the southern part of the park, although both the Ura and the Tana rivers have plenty of hippo.The photographs displayed in the lodge of a 24-hour fight to the finish between a python and a crocodile should provide sufficient encouragement to undertake this adventure trek in the hope of seeing an equally extraordinary event.

Doum palms are the dominant tree of the area, and along the banks of all the major streams and in the northeastern area one can see open grassland dotted with doums. The raphia palm is instantly recognizable with its magnificent 10-metre, mahogany-red branches.

At least two nights should be spent in Meru, as there is so much to see and do. The game is not as prolific as in, say, the Masai Mara, but there is a lot more satisfaction in finding game when it is scarce than when it stretches as far as the eye can see. Those who think that wildlife has become tamed in the parks will quickly learn the truth in Meru. Moreover, the different ecological environments you will discover, if you stay longer than a day, will provide other rewards. You might, for example, be tempted to think about the smaller, less obvious creatures.

On a safari through Kenya you cannot miss seeing a dung beetle at work. Despite its not very attractive name, this little animal is a close relative of the sacred scarab of ancient Egypt. You may see one busily preparing a ball of dung with its front legs and then propelling the finished ball with its hind ones. Despite being unable to see where it is going, not even the direction, it manages to move the dung ball to a safe place where it can bury the ball and itself. The beetle will then feast on the booty until it is completely consumed. When the mood takes it the beetle will select dung that is especially moist. Instead of rolling the ball away, it bores a hole in which it lays a single egg. Within a week the larva has hatched and finds itself alone in a world made of food. It eats its way through the surrounding supply, leaving only a hard, dry shell on the outside. Next it pupates, and a month later the dung beetle emerges. The first thing it does is to break out of its prison and head for the nearest droppings. It makes the inevitable ball and takes it away to eat. A true full circle.

The cicada is another small creature that spends a good deal of its life under-ground. No one leaves Africa without hearing the song of the cicada. Only the males make the distinctive sounds that are so elusive in origin. Females do not have the hollow drums, called timbals, on either side of the abdomen that are used for producing the song. The tightly stretched skin over the timbals is contracted and expanded by muscles, producing a sound in much the same way that a can does if you push the lid in and out. Cicadas lay their eggs in the bark of trees. As soon as a nymph appears it descends and buries itself, feeding on the juice of roots for two or three years. When fully mature, it emerges and climbs back into a tree. Very soon its mantle splits and an adult cicada appears. The adult feeds from the tree juices, extracting them by a battery of fine needles that take the place of a mouth.

All of these tiny scenes are part of the gigantic mosaic that is the wilderness. Meru is as good a place as any to marvel at nature's creations.

ACCOMMODATION

Meru Mulika Lodge (132 beds, 3 stars)

■ SELF-HELP
Leopard Rock Bandas (10 rooms)

Doum palm (Hyphaene compressa), *Meru National Park*

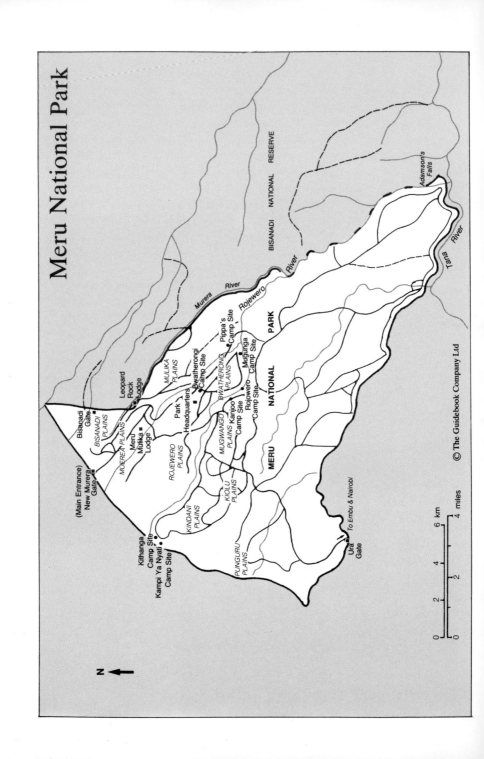

Meru National Park

Bird World

Kenya is blessed with an immense variety and uncountable numbers of birds. They are found in almost every district of the country and are numerous even in the cities. One gets the impression that Kenya is one big aviary. The authoritative guide is the *Checklist of the Birds of Kenya* by P L Britton et al, published in 1980 by the East African Natural History Society. Nevertheless, the average birdwatcher and certainly most visitors will be content with Collins' *Field Guide to the Birds of East and Central Africa* by John G Williams. An eminently 'pocketable' reference book.

On a serious bird safari, a dedicated 'twitcher' can expect to identify well over 400 species. The bird enthusiast should certainly try to join a safari planned by people who specialize in such trips.

The national parks and reserves of Kenya enjoy their own quotas of bird species, but they do not have a monopoly. There are many habitats outside the parks that are similar to those found inside them; and while mammals may be absent, birds may be plentiful. The lakes of the Rift Valley, particularly **Lake Magadi**, **Lake Naivasha** and **Lake Baringo**, are good examples. Bird safari specialists, therefore, do not necessarily follow routes through the national park and reserve networks but take their clients to a number of different ecological zones, of which seven are described here.

First, there are the **forests and moorlands**, found on Mount Kenya, Mount Elgon, the Aberdare Range and the Cheranganis, which themselves can be divided into three separate zones—highland forest, bamboo forest, and Afro-Alpine moorland. In these areas, quite a number of rare birds can be found, among them the green ibis, rufous-breasted sparrow hawk and the crowned eagle. The latter preys on a variety of animals, including baboons, monkeys, antelopes and even monitor lizards. Other interesting birds at these altitudes are the bronze-naped pigeon, Hartlaub's turaco, white-headed wood hoopoe, Alpine chat, slender-billed chestnut-winged starling, and fine-banded woodpecker. There are no less than 13 species of sunbirds, such as the golden-winged, tacazze, northern double-collared and the scarlet-tufted malachite, which nests in the dead leaves of the giant *Senecio johnstonii*.

A second habitat is the **lowland forest**, of which there is very little in Kenya; the only true examples are the Gede and the Sokoke-Arabuku forests near Malindi. These are home to many rare and local birds. Clearly local are the Sokoke scops owl and the Sokoke pipit, but Clarke's weaver has also only been located in Sokoke. Fischer's turaco, Retz's and chestnut-fronted helmet shrikes, the green barbet, the green tinkerbird and the dainty little yellow flycatcher are other rarer birds of this small region.

If you do visit the Sokoke Forest, you should try to spot the yellow-rumped elephant shrew that is reasonably common here but rare elsewhere. This interesting animal is quite large, about 45 centimetres (18 inches) in length, and has a huge and

(clockwise) *lesser flamingos, Lake Bogoria;*
heron, Lake Naivasha; Egyptian goose and
crowned crane; crowned crane, Masai Mara

distinctive proboscis. Even more difficult to spot is the Zanzibar (or Aders') duiker, which in Kenya is only found in Sokoke.

The **savannah bushlands** are typically the predominant landscapes in Samburu, Meru and Tsavo national parks. All these parks have large rivers flowing through them and the stands of tall acacias along the banks attract many bird species. Notable birds to look for in such areas are the ostrich and many birds of prey, including the martial eagle, pale-chanting goshawk, African hawk eagle and several species of vulture. Conspicuous, too, are vulturine guinea fowl, kori and buff-crested bustards, chestnut-bellied and black-faced sandgrouse, green wood hoopoe, yellow-bellied eremomela, and a multitude of weavers, waxbills and starlings. Among the last are golden-breasted starlings, arguably the most beautiful of a spectacular group of birds.

Next are the **savannah grasslands**, typified by the Masai Mara. Interesting species include the secretary bird, wattled plover, yellow-throated sandgrouse, lilac-breasted roller, ground hornbill, and masses of larks, pipits and widowbirds. In the dense riverine forest along the Mara River are several rare species, including Ross's and Livingstone's turacos, blue flycatcher, double-toothed barbet, and if you are lucky, Pel's fishing owl.

The fifth habitat centres around the **fresh and alkaline lakes**. Four of the lakes in the southern part of Kenya's Rift Valley are alkaline, and of these Lakes Nakuru and Bogoria are frequently the home of up to a million flamingos. Most are lesser flamingo, but greater flamingo also occur in far smaller numbers. Although other species of water birds are attracted by the alkaline lakes, the great majority prefer the freshwater lakes of Naivasha and Baringo. Over 400 species have been recorded at each of these lakes, and include white and pink-backed pelican, cormorant and the long-tailed cormorant, little bittern, goliath heron, purple heron, squacco heron, little, yellow and great white egrets, Allen's and purple gallinules, African spoonbills, jacana, and pied and malachite kingfishers. Large numbers of migrant waders and ducks can be seen during the northern hemisphere's winter.

The **desert and semi-desert**, especially the area around Lake Turkana, is the habitat of some extremely localized birds. These include Heuglin's bustard, Lichtenstein's sandgrouse, Abyssinian roller, brown-necked raven Somali fiscal, Somali sparrow, and the shining sunbird. Larks are represented by masked, crested and William's bush lark.

Last but not least is the **rain forest**. Kenya has an 'island' of rain forest at Kakamega, which was once part of the vast forest that covers much of Zaire and Uganda. Many birds not found elsewhere in Kenya are resident here. Among them are the grey parrot, great blue turaco, blue-headed bee-eater, black-and-white casqued hornbill, hairy-breasted barbet, brown-eared and yellow-crested woodpeckers and several of the Illadopsis group. You may also spot yellow-bellied wattle-eyes, pink-footed puffback, red-headed bluebill and the oriole finch.

The Coral Coast

Most visitors spend at least some of their time at Kenya's coast, on the Indian Ocean. In fact, among visitors to Kenya, sun-worshippers greatly outnumber safari enthusiasts. The Kenya coast is a good place to find the three main ingredients of a beach holiday: sea, sun and sand. The Indian Ocean is warm and balmy, at times azure and at other times opal. The whole of the 500 kilometres (312 miles) of coastline is protected by a fringing reef, so not only are there no sharks but there are myriads of fishes in party dresses suspended amongst the coral gardens. Several marine parks and reserves have been created to protect this spectacular underwater wonderland.

Mombasa

Mombasa is the centre of the coast, and is Kenya's second largest town as well as its only port. Visitors arrive at Mombasa either at the Moi International airport, 12 kilometres (eight miles) from the town centre, or by the overnight train from Nairobi, which arrives in downtown Mombasa in the early morning. Few drive from Nairobi to Mombasa as the journey of 485 kilometres (305 miles) takes some six hours of concentrated driving, and the second half tends to be rather boring as far as scenery is concerned. Some companies offer tours that terminate in Mombasa, having passed through Tsavo on the way. This is an infinitely better way to tackle the road journey, and has the added advantage that you return by a less arduous means.

There has been a town at Mombasa for at least ten centuries, nine more than at Nairobi. The town definitely looks a little worn, a little uncared for, and redolent of Somerset Maugham or Graham Greene. Despite this aura of decay, the streets are bustling and the atmosphere vibrant. You hardly ever see a collar and tie and if you do, it belongs to an itinerant trader from Nairobi. The local people have learned how to live in a hot and often humid climate. They dress in loose clothes, often shunning trousers for a loose *kikoi* or *khanga*, both of them lengths of cotton tied around the waist and worn in the manner of a skirt.

The majority of people inhabiting the coastal littoral are Muslims and the influence of Islam is obvious. Men wear the *kofia*, a small, often richly embroidered cap, and many women still wrap themselves in the black robe-like *buibui*. Less than a century ago, many women walked under a cotton tent held erect by servants and were thus completely concealed from men's gazes. Now the veil is hardly seen in the city centre but it still prevails in the Old Town. For a casual visitor the Old Town holds much more fascination than the modern section where, apart from a few streets with some interesting shopping for souvenirs (Moi Avenue, Digo Road and Biashara

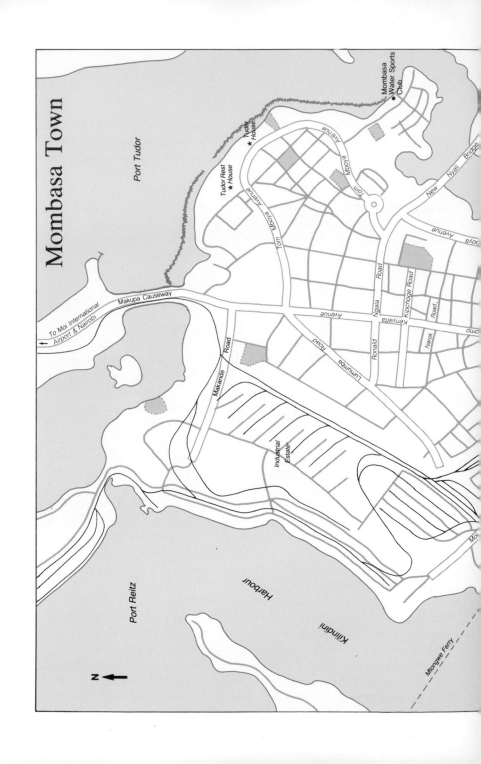

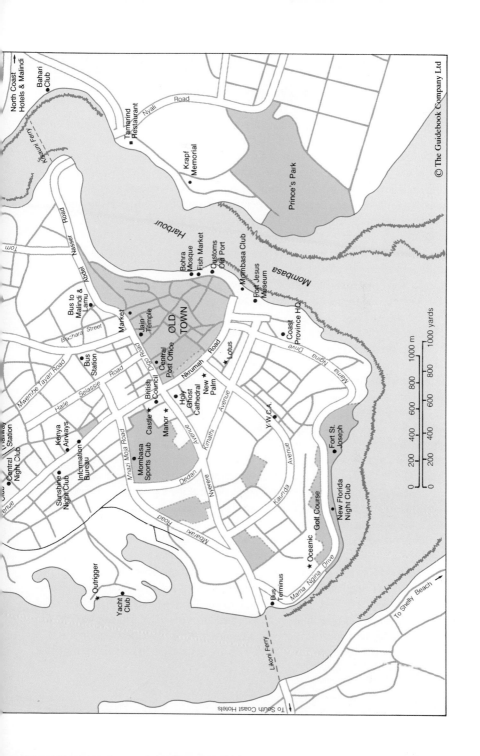

North Coast
Hotels & Malindi →

Bahari
Club

Kilauri Ferry

Tamarind
Restaurant

Nyali   Road

Krapf
Memorial

Prince's Park

Harbour

Mombasa

Tom

Nasser   Road

Abdel

Bohra
Mosque
Fish Market
Customs
Old Port

Mombasa Club

Bus to
Malindi &
Lamu

Biashara Street

Market

Jain
Temple

OLD
TOWN

Fort Jesus
Museum

Bus
Station

Digo Road

Central
Post Office

Nkrumah   Road

Lotus

Coast
Province HQ

Mwembe Tayari Road

Solassie   Road

Halle

British
Council

Holy
Ghost
Cathedral

New
Palm

Avenue

Avenue

Mama Ngina   Drive

Kenya
Airways

Castle

Manor

Kimathi

Y.W.C.A.

Central
Night Club

Information
Bureau

Mnazi Moja Road

Mombasa
Sports Club

Dedan

Avenue

Nyerere

Avenue

Fort St.
Joseph

Sunshine
Night Club

Kaunda

0   200   400   600   800   1000 m

New Florida
Night Club

Mbaraki   Road

Oceanic
Golf Course

0   200   400   600   800   1000 yards

Outrigger

Yacht
Club

Bus
Terminus

Mama Ngina   Drive

Likoni Ferry

To South Coast Hotels

To Shelly Beach

© The Guidebook Company Ltd

Street), the town seems full of nothing but men's clothing shops and travel and tour agencies.

The Old Town, a maze of narrow streets scarcely two paces across, centres on the old harbour. It is roughly triangular in shape, its base the line of the sea and its sides stretching from Fort Jesus in the south and Abdel Nasser Road in the north to an apex where Digo and Makadara roads meet. *Ndia Kuu*, which in Swahili means 'the High Street', runs from the Fort to *Mlango wa Papa*, 'the Shark's Entrance', an area where *dhows* are careened when they visit during the northeast monsoon. But few come here these days, so the *dhow* harbour is no longer the splendid sight it once was.

Mbarak Ali Hinawy Street, which runs directly from the fort, past the Mombasa Club with its heavy colonial overtones, to Government Square at the *dhow* harbour, is named after Sir Mbarak, an author, historian, and the last but one *Liwali* of the coast appointed by the then colonial government. This post, largely honorific, nevertheless had certain legal powers. Just beyond the Custom House is the new Burhani Bohra Mosque, the third mosque to be built on this site by the Bohra community. Just beyond the mosque is Leven House, named after a British ship that in 1824 put ashore one Lieutenant Reitz as administrator of a short-lived protectorate. Reitz himself is remembered at Port Reitz, an area of water near Mombasa airport and beyond the main harbour of Kilindini.

Just beyond the Leven House and the Leven Steps is a perfume shop, well worth a visit if only to see the enormous Portuguese wine 'Old Large Jar'. The owner sells 'all the perfumes of Araby', plus many more from Kashmir, and still uses an Indian measure called a *tola*, which was the weight of a rupee. There are lots of enchanting shops in the Old Town, besides the inevitable multitude of curio shops, including some silver- and goldsmiths, and the row of spice shops at the top of Langoni Road near the MacKinnon Market should not be missed. That market, too, is interesting; you will see a range of fruits and vegetables you did not know existed.

Dominating the Old Town, and a must on any tour of Mombasa, is **Fort Jesus**, once the symbol of Portuguese hegemony and since 1958 a museum. Built in the last years of the 16th century by an Italian architect, its wide corner bastions reflect this origin. In 1631, the Portuguese garrison was surprised and overrun by an Arab army of the Sultan of Mombasa. The Portuguese recaptured the fort a year later only to lose it again in 1698, this time to the armies of the Sultan of Oman. The fort was turned into a barracks for Omani soldiers and a residence for the Omani governor. It was recovered by the Portuguese in 1728 and finally abandoned 18 months later for lack of food.

Mombasa, 1929, with Arab traders in situ

In 1746, the Arab governor, Ali bin Othman of the Mazrui family, declared his independence of the Omani sultan. There followed a long struggle between the Iman and the Mazrui governors of Mombasa, Lamu and Pate, until they were finally quelled by Seyyid Said bin Sultan in 1837. It was in the final stages of this struggle that Suleiman bin Ali, then governor of Mombasa, enlisted British aid to declare the short-lived protectorate of which Lieutenant Reitz was the administrator. This protectorate was not to last, as the British government declined to recognize it. No major structural changes were made during the Arab occupation of Fort Jesus, although the chapel became a mosque. Even the inscriptions and coats of arms of the Portuguese were left intact and still can be read today. The Arabs added to the inscriptions, and the six beams in the mosque are all inscribed. One has a verse that, translated, reads:

> Endure all bitterness of insult. Perhaps it may disappear. Should things twist and entangle, God's Command comes down from heaven and unravels them.

In 1875, the commander of the sultan's troops, Al Akida, tried to burn down the town of Mombasa, then barricaded himself in the fort, until he was dislodged by two British ships, the *Nassau* and the *Rifleman*. Damage to the northeast bastion and the house behind the gun platform, caused by the ships' gunfire, is still visible. In 1895, when the coastal strip became a British protectorate, the sultan's garrison withdrew to

Zanzibar and the fort became a prison. It remained so until it was transformed into a museum in 1958 with the help of a grant from the Gulbenkian Foundation. The museum within the fort now houses a collection of coastal relics dating back to the ninth century. Also on view are some of the artefacts raised from the wreck of the *Santo Antonio de Tanna*, which sank near the fort in 1697 while attempting to raise the siege.

A less esoteric attraction near Mombasa town, in the suburb of **Nyali**, is **Mamba Village**, said to be the 'world's largest crocodile farm'. Despite the hype, it is worth a visit. Not far away from Mamba Village is Kenya's own 'safari park'. Just north of Mombasa along the road to Malindi

Indian Temple, Mombasa, its Ganesha god well to the fore

you cannot escape seeing the monstrous Bamburi Cement Works, surrounded by a desert of its own making. Yet a new world has been brought into existence by the creators of this desolation. The owners of the cement works engaged the services of René Haller, a renowned agronomist, who transformed 35 hectares (86 acres) of limestone pits into the **Bamburi Nature Trail**, a sublime garden of forest, glades, pools and streams. Here are found eland, oryx, waterbuck, bush pig, crocodile, monkeys and hippo; and birds, too, in great profusion.

Back in Mombasa town you can visit the **carvers' village**, not far from the airport. Hundreds of woodcarvers stay here, transforming the roughest logs into articles of grace and beauty. They demonstrate their skills using apparently antique, some might think prehistoric tools. This is actually a co-operative and you can buy from the village shop when you have had enough of walking around.

By now you will have seen the important parts of Mombasa, except perhaps the giant tusks that span the town's main road, Moi Avenue. These were originally erected as part of the welcome for Britain's Princess Margaret when she visited the town in 1956. Originally made of canvas stretched on wood, they were such a success that they were re-created later in aluminium as a permanent landmark.

The Kenya Coast, like Gaul, is divided into three parts. These are the South Coast, the North Coast, and Malindi/Watamu.

Shoe maker, Biashara Street

THE EXPLORERS

Johann Ludwig Krapf was born in Germany in 1810. He entered the Mission College in Basle at the age of 17, and ten years later went to Ethiopia on behalf of the Church Missionary Society. After six years there, thwarted by Copt and Catholic, he felt that his limited success with the Galla of the south could be better furthered by approaching these people from the East African coast and from territory not ruled by the Ethiopian princes. Before doing so, he travelled to Cairo to wed a lady he had not met. They sailed south in a variety of *dhows* to reach Zanzibar in January 1844. In March, with Rosine now pregnant, they left for Mombasa armed with a *laissez-passer* from the Sultan of Zanzibar: 'This comes from Seyyid Said Sultan. Greetings to all our subjects, friends and Governors. This letter is written on behalf of Dr Krapf, the German, a good man who wishes to convert the world to God. Behave well to him, and be everywhere serviceable to him.' Rosine, stricken with fever, gave birth to a daughter on 6 July and died three days later. By 15 July the baby was also dead. A less resourceful man would have packed up and gone home. On the contrary, Johann travelled inland exploring and seeking the right place to build his mission station. The CMS agreed to send him an assistant, and in 1846 **Johann Rebmann** arrived.

The two men built their mission at Rabai, near Mombasa, a base from which they intended to spread Christianity inland. On his second expedition inland, Rebmann recorded in his diary, 'This morning we discerned the mountains of Jagga more distinctly... and about ten o'clock, I fancied I saw the summit of one of them covered in a dazzling white cloud. My guide called the white which I saw, merely "baredi", cold; it was perfectly clear to me, however, that it could be nothing else but snow.' Later, while resting, he read Psalm 111 and the promise in verse 6 'made a lasting impression on me'. It reads, 'He hath shewed his people the power of his works, that he may give them the heritage of the heathen.' Thus Rebmann was the first European to set eyes on the snows of Kilimanjaro. It was Krapf who was first to see the snows of Mount Kenya. On the 3 December 1849, he 'could see the Kegnia most distinctly and observed two horns or pillars, as it were, rising over an enormous mountain...covered with a white substance.' Kegnia was Krapf's rendering of the local Kamba name *Kinyaa*, from which later British colonists coined the name Kenya.

The reports of snow on the Equator, and of a great inland sea, inspired interested parties in Europe to undertake 'professional' explorations. **Burton** and **Speke** arrived in 1856 to test the accuracy of the reports, and in 1858, Speke reached the southern shore of the 'inland sea', which the Arab traders called *Ukerewe*, and renamed it Victoria Nyanza.

In 1863, the **Reverend Charles New** arrived in East Africa as a Methodist missionary. He became the first European to climb Mount Kilimanjaro to the snowline, in August 1871.

In 1883, **Joseph Thomson** was sent by the Royal Geographical Society to try to discover a short route to the northern end of Lake Victoria, through 'the country of the Masai'. Fifteeen months later he returned to Rabai, having achieved all he set out to do. 'Half an hour sufficed to bring us to the top of a low range of hills, and there lay the end of our pilgrimage—a glistening bay of the Great Lake surrounded by low shore...the view...could not be called picturesque, though it was certainly pleasing. Next day I rested from my labours with the delicious consciousness that a great feat had been accomplished and that I had home as the new beacon-star ahead to direct my wandering footsteps.' Later, he and his companion James Martin, a Maltese, 'laid aside our natural reserve, and packeting our high dignity...illustrated [to the local people] the "poetry of motion" as practised in Malta and Scotland; that is to say, Martin tried to initiate the damsels into the mysterious charm of the waltz while I showed them how to do the "fantastic" in the spirited movements of a Scotch dance.'

Four years later, in 1887, **Samuel Teleki von Szek**, a count of the Holy Roman Empire, then aged 42, accompanied by **Lieutenant von Hohnel**, left the East African coast to explore the northern areas of what is now Kenya and to search for the lakes north of Lake Baringo that Thompson had mentioned in his published account of his journey, *Through Masai Land*. Climbing to the glaciers of Mount Kenya on the way (and leaving the 'Teleki Valley' as a memorial), they marched through Samburu country, naming the 'Mathews Range' after General Lloyd Mathews, the commander of the Sultan of Zanzibar's army. In February 1888, they reached *Basso Narok*, the Black Lake, and renamed it Rudolf after the Crown Prince of Austria. Reaching the northern end of the lake (having passed through Koobi Fora, where the now famous hominid discoveries were made 80 years later), they were confronted by tribesmen who would not allow them to continue westward to complete the exploration of the western shores of the lake. They did, however, manage to reach *Basso Ebor,* the White Lake (more properly *Empaso Naibor*), which was anything but white and on whose 'beach and in the air were thousands of scavenger birds, including vultures, marabout storks and crows, glutting themselves with the fish that lay about in great quantities in various stages of decomposition. The water of the lake was very brackish.' Teleki named the lake in honour of Prince Rudolf's wife, the Archduchess Stefanie. Most of Lake Stefanie now lies in Ethiopia, but a muddy extension crosses the border into Kenya and its name has been changed to Lake Chew Bahir.

The last of the explorers was **Dr John Walter Gregory**, a Londoner born in 1864. In 1893, he undertook a journey from Mombasa to explore and report on the geology of the East African part...'of the valley which runs from the Lebanon almost to the Cape'. Many geographers had described the great trough that split Africa almost from end to end but it was left to Gregory to define its origins. After much harassment from the Masai, and finding himself in the midst of constant warfare between them and the Kikuyu, he moved to the area of Lake Baringo. There he was able to analyse the strata

from top to bottom of the eastern wall, the Laikipia escarpment, carefully noting where he found his specimens and at what height. He moved to the western side where the tilted Tugen Hills revealed information about the upturned strata. He did not complete his examination of the Elgeyo escarpment, which is actually the western wall of the rift in that area, but returned to England and announced that 'these valleys were not formed by removal, grain by grain, by rivers or wind, of the rocks which originally occupied

The glaciated summit of Kilimanjaro

them, but by the rock sinking in mass, while the adjacent land remained stationary....For this type of valley I suggest the name Rift Valley, using the term rift in the sense of a relatively narrow space due to subsidence between parallel fractures. Such valleys are known in many parts of the world, but that of East Africa may justly be called the Great Rift Valley.'

The South Coast

The South Coast refers to the area from Mombasa south to the Tanzanian border. Most Kenyans, and probably most tour operators, rate the South Coast the best in the country, but they are really referring to **Diani Beach**, near Ukunda in the centre of the South Coast. There are in fact several better beaches, but they are little known and therefore not developed. If a resort is what you want, Diani Beach is certainly your best choice. Apart from Diani there is a small development at **Likoni**, just after the ferry that connects Mombasa island to the south mainland. Here is **Shelley Beach Hotel**, the nearest beach hotel to the town centre.

Before you reach Diani Beach, which is 35 kilometres (22 miles) from Mombasa, you come to **Tiwi Beach**, actually a number of small sandy beaches divided by coral outcrops. At low tide the water is very shallow here and you can walk out to the reef. By Sand Island, which is a permanent but shifting island, there is some good snorkelling. Most of the accommodation at Tiwi is in the form of cottages for rental grouped in villages; some of these have a restaurant attached, and all will find you a cook if you are thinking of a self-catering holiday.

Not far past Tiwi you come to Ukunda and you turn left here for Diani Beach. This is a textbook tropical beach, with wide, white sands and quivering palm trees. It is relatively crowded by Kenyan standards but that means quite empty by European ones. There are a series of first-rate hotels here, wonderfully comfortable and reasonably priced. An added attraction of this stretch of beach is the attractive forest that separates it from the highway. Although much of the forest is giving way to development (if that is the correct word), remnants still conceal monkeys, including colobus, and a dazzle of brilliant birds.

Another delight is the **Kongo Mosque** near the north end of the beach, where a new hotel, the Indian Ocean Beach Club, has just opened. The 15th-century mosque, recently partially restored, is the only example of a barrel-vaulted roof along the entire coast.

All the hotels provide evening entertainment of the sort usually found in resorts. There are two casinos, one at **Leopard Beach** and the other at **Leisure Lodge**. Two speciality restaurants stand out. One is **Ali Barbour's** built into a limestone cave, and therefore both curious and a trifle bizarre, but the food is good. Try also **Vulcanos**, elegant and Italian.

For good snorkelling you have to go a little farther afield. An interesting day out

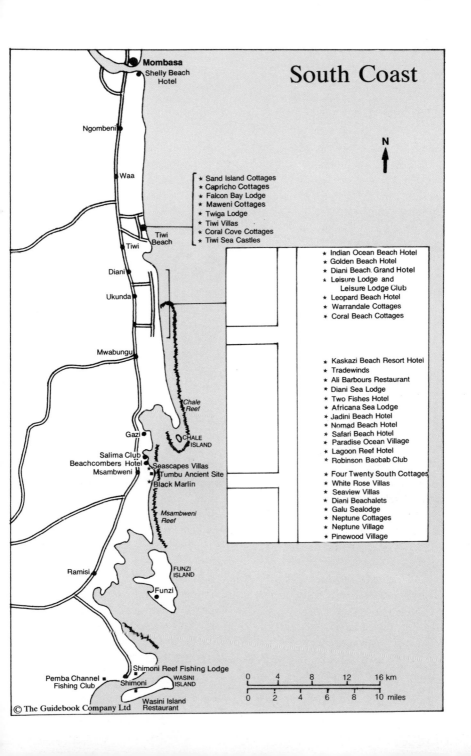

South Coast

Mombasa
Shelly Beach Hotel

Ngombeni

Waa

★ Sand Island Cottages
★ Capricho Cottages
★ Falcon Bay Lodge
★ Maweni Cottages
★ Twiga Lodge
★ Tiwi Villas
★ Coral Cove Cottages
★ Tiwi Sea Castles

Tiwi Beach
Tiwi

Diani

Ukunda

★ Indian Ocean Beach Hotel
★ Golden Beach Hotel
★ Diani Beach Grand Hotel
★ Leisure Lodge and Leisure Lodge Club
★ Leopard Beach Hotel
★ Warrandale Cottages
★ Coral Beach Cottages

Mwabungu

★ Kaskazi Beach Resort Hotel
★ Tradewinds
★ Ali Barbours Restaurant
★ Diani Sea Lodge
★ Two Fishes Hotel
★ Africana Sea Lodge
★ Jadini Beach Hotel
★ Nomad Beach Hotel
★ Safari Beach Hotel
★ Paradise Ocean Village
★ Lagoon Reef Hotel
★ Robinson Baobab Club

Chale Reef

Gazi

CHALE ISLAND

Salima Club
Beachcombers Hotel
Msambweni

Seascapes Villas
Tumbu Ancient Site
Black Marlin

★ Four Twenty South Cottages
★ White Rose Villas
★ Seaview Villas
★ Diani Beachalets
★ Galu Sealodge
★ Neptune Cottages
★ Neptune Village
★ Pinewood Village

Msambweni Reef

Ramisi

FUNZI ISLAND

Funzi

Shimoni Reef Fishing Lodge

Pemba Channel Fishing Club
Shimoni

WASINI ISLAND

Wasini Island Restaurant

0   4   8   12   16 km

0   2   4   6   8   10 miles

N

© The Guidebook Company Ltd

is to take Nomad Safaris' daily boat trip to **Chale Island**. You have a snorkelling session on the way and then a fish BBQ on the beach. Almost all the hotels have a sea sports centre, where you can hire windsurfers, learn scuba-diving, or (in the north-eastern monsoon) try para-sailing. Further south from Diani the coast attracts travellers rather than tourists, and deep-sea fishermen as well. For a delightful get-away-from-it-all spot try Salima at **Msambweni**. This is a designer self-catering complex, fully serviced (if that isn't a contradiction). You rent the villa and when you arrrive you find all the food you will need for a day or two in the fridge and in the larder. You also find smiling staff assigned to make your self-catering holiday a holiday without the self-catering. *Msambweni* means 'the place of the sable antelope'. Nowadays, this noble animal is found only in the **Shimba Hills National Reserve**, which dominates the coastal plains. But more of that later.

Farther south, and quite near the border, is **Shimoni**, whose name means 'the place of the hole'. The 'hole' is a series of huge limestone caves that were once used as slave prisons. The cries of the unfortunate prisoners still haunt the eerie interiors. At Shimoni is the **Pemba Channel Fishing Club**, whose domain reaches into the Mozambique Channel. It is said to be the finest fishing along the East African coast. You need to book well ahead, for the place is small and it has its dedicated aficionados.

Shimoni is also the starting point for a visit to the **Kisite Mpunguti Marine Park and Reserve**. Scarcely anywhere in the world can beat the snorkelling around the small islet of Kisite. The journey there in a *dhow*, followed by a seafood lunch on the island of Wasini, makes just one of those days you remember for a lifetime. Getting there involves quite a lot of effort, for it is little visited—a fact that makes it even better when *you* go there.

A few miles inland are the Shimba Hills. These rise to about 500 metres (1,600 feet) and offer a cool haven from the heat of the beaches. They also offer, within the **Shimba Hills National Reserve**, the chance to see the most dramatic of the antelope family, the sable. Few sights in the animal kingdom can rival the splendour of the male sable with his enormous scimitar-shaped horns. There are also roan antelope in the reserve, so make sure you identify them correctly. A splendid little tree hotel, **Shimba Hills Lodge**, nestles in the forest overlooking a waterhole where elephant and leopard pause to drink. There are wonderful views of the coast littoral from these hills, and if you achieve nothing else (for the game is by no means prolific) the vistas are worth the journey.

Dhows *on the coast*

The North Coast

The destination called the North Coast stretches some 30 kilometres (20 miles) from Mombasa island as far as **Kikambala**. Along this coastline are five beaches where almost all the hotels are found. You leave Mombasa by the new Nyali Bridge (it was new in 1987, but is still called new). On your right is Mombasa's garden suburb, **Nyali**, and on your left **Freretown**, a rather crowded suburb originally set up to house freed slaves, and even now the home of many of their descendants. The corner of the road leading to Nyali, on your right, is decorated with a bell tower that belongs to the church on your left, but has been separated by the new road. The Emmanuel Church is the second oldest in Kenya and was built by freed slaves in 1884. Inside is a picture of Matthew Wellington, who is buried near the church. He was one of the people sent to find Livingstone and who carried his body all the way from Ujiji on Lake Tanganyika to the coast.

The first of the north coast beaches is **Nyali Beach**, a fine stretch of shimmering white sand shaded by thousands of palms. The oldest beach hotel in Kenya is the Nyali Beach Hotel, now much modernized and still extremely popular. A small headland separates Nyali from **Mombasa Beach**, where there are five attractive hotels. This beach has all the attributes of the archetypal tropical strand: shady palms, soft white sand between the toes, and a warm oystershell sea. There is, of course, a reef protecting the calm lagoons from predators. The waters between the beach and the reef are alive with boats, varying from the local dugout with outriggers—the *ngalawa* —to deep-sea fishing vessels.

Beyond Mombasa Beach is **Kenyatta Beach**, one of the very few public beaches in the country and well sprinkled with hotels in the middle price range. **Shanzu Beach**, which is next, has a steeper slope to the sea, thus offering the possibility of swimming at middle and low tides. Serena Beach Hotel and the Mombasa Inter-Continental are situated on this beach.

A little beyond Shanzu you come to **Mtwapa Creek**, spanned by yet another 'new' bridge and a good place to rent a house if you want to be away from the bustle and glare of the ocean. On the beach on the north side of the creek is a small ruined town called **Jumba la Mtwana**, 'the slavemaster's mansion'. This is a jewel of a monument, and if you only visit one historic site on your Kenya holiday then make this high up on the priority list. It is a splendid shady site for a picnic and the ruins are sufficiently preserved to bring the site to life. One of its splendid mosques is slipping inexorably into the advancing sands. Near this mosque are some tombs, one of which is inscribed 'Every soul shall taste death. You will simply be paid your wages in full on the

North Coast, Malindi & Watamu

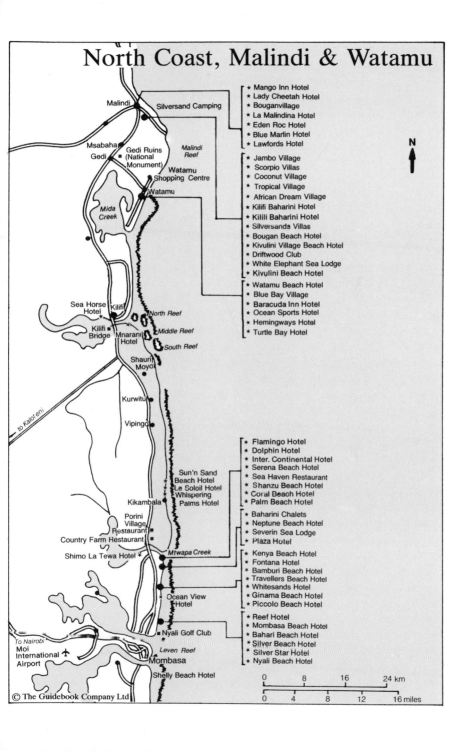

Malindi

Silversand Camping

Msabaha
Gedi

Gedi Ruins
(National
Monument)

Malindi
Reef

Watamu
Shopping Centre

Watamu

Mida
Creek

Sea Horse
Hotel

Kilifi

North Reef

Kilifi
Bridge

Mnarani
Hotel

Middle Reef

South Reef

Shauri
Moyo

Kurwitu

Vipingo

Sun'n Sand
Beach Hotel
Le Soloil Hotel
Whispering
Palms Hotel

Kikambala

Porini
Village
Restaurant

Country Farm Restaurant

Shimo La Tewa Hotel

Mtwapa Creek

Ocean View
Hotel

Nyali Golf Club

To Nairobi
Moi
International
Airport

Leven Reef

Mombasa

Shelly Beach Hotel

to Kaloleni

N

★ Mango Inn Hotel
★ Lady Cheetah Hotel
★ Bouganvillage
★ La Malindina Hotel
★ Eden Roc Hotel
★ Blue Marlin Hotel
★ Lawfords Hotel

★ Jambo Village
★ Scorpio Villas
★ Coconut Village
★ Tropical Village
★ African Dream Village
★ Kilifi Baharini Hotel
★ Kilili Baharini Hotel
★ Silversands Villas
★ Bougan Beach Hotel
★ Kivulini Village Beach Hotel
★ Driftwood Club
★ White Elephant Sea Lodge
★ Kivulini Beach Hotel

★ Watamu Beach Hotel
★ Blue Bay Village
★ Baracuda Inn Hotel
★ Ocean Sports Hotel
★ Hemingways Hotel
★ Turtle Bay Hotel

★ Flamingo Hotel
★ Dolphin Hotel
★ Inter. Continental Hotel
★ Serena Beach Hotel
★ Sea Haven Restaurant
★ Shanzu Beach Hotel
★ Coral Beach Hotel
★ Palm Beach Hotel

★ Baharini Chalets
★ Neptune Beach Hotel
★ Severin Sea Lodge
★ Plaza Hotel

★ Kenya Beach Hotel
★ Fontana Hotel
★ Bamburi Beach Hotel
★ Travellers Beach Hotel
★ Whitesands Hotel
★ Ginama Beach Hotel
★ Piccolo Beach Hotel

★ Reef Hotel
★ Mombasa Beach Hotel
★ Bahari Beach Hotel
★ Silver Beach Hotel
★ Silver Star Hotel
★ Nyali Beach Hotel

0		8		16		24 km
0	4		8		12	16 miles

Day of Resurrection.' A small guidebook is available at the entrance.

Continuing for ten kilometres (six miles) past Mtwapa, on the main Malindi road you come to **Kikambala Beach**. This is another attractive place, with only two hotels, both of which are considerably cheaper than their equivalents on beaches nearer to Mombasa. There are also some cottages for rent here.

Watamu and Malindi

Heading north after Kikambala you pass the huge Vipingo Sisal Estate, where sisal has been grown since 1934. The plant *Agave sisalana* originated in Mexico and is cultivated for the fibre produced from its leaves. You may see some tall spikes five or six metres (15–20 feet) high. These are the 'flowers' that are produced when the plant is about seven or eight years old. If allowed to mature, the pole will produce up to 2,000 bulbils, by which the plant reproduces. Leaving the estate, you see a sign to Takaungu, a delightful as-it-always-was village with no tourists. There is a small, enchanting beach, some fisherfolk and some ghosts. Most people who see and hear the ghosts think they are reminders of slaves, for they hear the clanking of chains. But there was also a revolt here against the administration of the Imperial East Africa Company, and it seems quite possible that it was put down with excessive and perhaps hideous force. Not far from Takaungu you come to **Kilifi Creek** and its new bridge. This one *is* new; it was completed in 1991. Before then a ferry plied the creek and was notorious for spending much of its time drifting half-way across. The ferry (or rather its absence) is one reason why the development of this stretch of coastline has lagged behind the other Kenyan resorts. **Watamu Beach** is the favourite of many Kenyans. The beach surrounds a crescent bay, in which are dotted a number of islets. One of these is shaped like a turtle, hence **Turtle Bay**.

Although beach holidays predominate, Watamu is also a prime deep-sea fishing locale, with Hemingway's hotel the focus. Here and Malindi are the centres for hunting sailfish, which ride these waters from November through March. The ocean around Watamu, as far as the reef, is a marine national park, while beyond the reef a national reserve extends five kilometres (three miles) seawards. The park is a fine place for underwater exploration. This is made easy by the hotels, all of which offer glass-bottomed boat trips to the coral gardens and from which you can snorkel and dive in a bafflingly beautiful world.

Near Watamu are two interesting sites. One is **Mida Creek**, a superlative place for birds, particularly waders and seabirds. Its underwater grottos are also the hideout of Kenya's biggest groupers, impossibly ugly fish, and harmless. Some are said to reach 300 kilograms (660 pounds). The other delight is **Gede** (sometimes **Gedi**), which is

Kenya's best preserved archeological treasure. Gede is definitely worth a visit. Situated in the remnants of lowland forest, it was once an important community, apparently founded in the 13th century and inexplicably vacated in the 17th century. It features in no known writings of the period, yet it was only a short distance from the then major sultanate at Malindi. Every other Swahili town was built on the coast, since the inhabitants had a maritime culture, except Gede, which lies six kilometres (four miles) from the sea and nearly the same distance from the nearest part of Mida Creek.

It was possibly the presence of fresh water that determined Gede's existence, and the drying-up of that supply the reason for its decline. More likely, the town was ransacked by a hostile tribe from the hinterland, the **Galla**, whose history of pillage from the Somali border southwards is well-documented. It is also possible that a cannibal tribe from southern Africa, the **Zimba**, reached Gede after they had assisted

Gede: these romantic ruins retain the secret of their sudden abandonment

the Portuguese in the capture of Mombasa in 1589. Gede is best visited in the late afternoon when it is cooler and when the light and shade enhance the mystery of this ruin. No one leaves Gede without experiencing its eerie, haunting ambience, which is enhanced by the encroaching forest, the silence and the majesty of a city devoid of life.There is a modern **Giriama** village at the entrance whose inhabitants dance and drum when visitors seem sufficient for an audience.

Sixteen kilometres (10 miles) from Gede lies **Malindi**. The town's origins are not known and the references in written history are in doubt up to the 13th century, when an Arab, Abu al Fida, described the location of a town so accurately that it must certainly be the present-day Malindi. In any event, we do know that in 1417 a Chinese delegation visited Malindi and were presented with a giraffe, which they took home by junk as a gift from the Sultan of Malindi to the Emperor of China. Eighty years later, in April 1498, Vasco Da Gama sailed into Malindi harbour and was given a great welcome by the sultan. At this time Malindi was a flourishing town, and apart from the local **Segeju** people, there were the immigrant Arab rulers and quite substantial numbers of traders from India. Inward trade consisted of cotton cloth, glass bottles, porcelain, beads and salt, while exports were largely ivory, cowries, rhino horn and ambergris. Surrounding the town were plantations of oranges and coconuts. Today, cotton is grown in quantity near Malindi and there is a huge sea-salt processing business at Fundisa, a few kilometres north of the town.

The first hotel in Malindi was the Palm Beach, built in 1931 on the site of what is now the Blue Marlin. Among its early visitors was Ernest Hemingway, who came to fish for marlin in 1934. Perhaps it was the celebrity status accorded to the town by Hemingway and his companion, Alfred Vanderbilt, that caused a Commander Lawford to build his hotel next to the Palm Beach. Lawford's hotel has been expanded and rebuilt several times since then. By the end of the 1940s, two more hotels had been added, and Malindi had become Kenya's premier (and only) holiday resort. Real expansion began in 1965 when the first charter flight from Europe arrived in Kenya. Another expansion took place in the second half of the 1980s, when there was a large influx of Italians, first as tourists and then as holiday home-owners and hoteliers. Today there are 1,750 tourist-class beds in the town and its immediate vicinity.

The wide sweep of Malindi Bay lost a great deal of its attraction in the mid-1970s when a sandbank burst. For centuries the sandbank had prevented the silt brought down the neighbouring Sabaki River from being deposited in the limpid waters of the bay. Now, from April through July, the bay may be too dirty for swimming. That same silt has a more beneficial action. Carried out to sea, it has prevented the coral on the reef from growing; the absence of a reef allows breakers to enter the bay and so surfing can take place. Malindi may not be the greatest surfing place in the world, but it has its devotees who come to the resort for that purpose instead of choosing other spots along the coast.

Next to Malindi Bay is **Silversands Bay**, where many of the new hotels have been built and which is free from silt year round. Just beyond Silversands is the access to the **Malindi Marine National Park** at Casuarina Point. The park itself is quite small, stretching out to sea for one and a half kilometres (one mile) and bounded in the south by Leopard Point, and in the north by Chanoni Point. The park is further protected by being within the Watamu Marine National Park, which starts at Mida Creek and ends just short of Malindi town. Two reefs are contained within the park, the North Reef and Barracuda Reef. At the southern end of North Reef are the famous Coral Gardens, where the water is shallow and usually crystal clear. Most of the fishes found along the coast and all of the coral types are found here. Brain coral predominates, and the colourful confusion of reef fishes is amazing. All this can easily be seen from the glass-bottomed boats that ply for hire at the park entrance, but if you are a good swimmer and can snorkel there is another fascination waiting for you here. At the end of the North Reef, near the Coral Gardens, the outer edge of the reef slopes steeply away 10–15 metres (30–45 feet) to a sandy bottom, which itself slopes less sharply to the channel. The coral fish give way to the pelagic fish, kingfish and kolekole in particular, but there are also unicorn fish and groupers and you will see lobsters waving to you from their coral cabins. You do not need to be a scuba diver to enjoy this spectacle, but you need to be a strong swimmer. You can get to this area from the glass-bottomed boat that anchors in the Coral Gardens.

Malindi has lost much of the Swahili ambience that in past times had been an attraction for the visitor. Now it grows daily more cosmopolitan and to some this may be welcome. There is a casino and a nightclub, the **Stardust**, has become well known. There are pizza gardens and ice-cream parlours and shopping centres and banks, but it is still Africa and there are still the delights that bring people here in the first place: the beaches and the magic of the sea, the bright sun, the balmy nights—and the urge to do nothing.

But for those visitors, fewer no doubt, who want to travel, to explore and to experience, then pass beyond Malindi to **Lamu**. The beach on Lamu Island is 12 kilometres (seven and a half miles) of empty sands backing on to an ocean unprotected by a reef and therefore more lively, more dynamic than you find elsewhere. But no one really comes to Lamu for the beach, at least not only for the beach. Lamu is a town, an island and an archipelago. If you visit Lamu you must visit all three. The archipelago is a chain of seven large islands and a multitude of islets, separated from the mainland by a channel that is just a few metres wide in places. The mainland and the inland sides of the islands are fringed with dense mangrove forests, while the seaward sides are protected by reefs and dunes. Throughout the archipelago there are numerous historical sites, visible and tangible evidence of ten centuries of a colourful and often violent past. Most of the settlements are Arab in origin and started as small

Lamu—a special blend of Arab and African culture

trading stations. As these small colonies grew, they absorbed much from the local people and a distinct Arab-African culture, now termed **Swahili**, emerged.

Lamu is reached by local scheduled air services from Mombasa, Malindi and Nairobi. A good road connects Malindi to Mkowe on the mainland; from there a 'water taxi' takes you to the island and the town. Mkowe is 225 kilometres (140 miles) from Malindi and there is a guarded car park where you can leave your car. There are buses twice a day that attract the adventurous, the robust and the less well-heeled, but even those with the first two qualities should be wary of accepting standing room in the bus.

When you arrive in Lamu town you enter a time warp and are back to somewhere around 1830. The town is crowded with houses and people, the streets so narrow that you can shake hands with your neighbour in the opposite house. There are very few dominant characteristics—perhaps the main street (like Mombasa's, called Ndia Kuu), which is slightly wider than most and which enables a donkey and cart to pass; these you have to avoid by taking refuge in a doorway. Otherwise, the fort stands out. Built by the Omanis around 1812 (or rather by local people under the direction of the Omanis), it is the centre of the town. Up to a few years ago, the fort was used as a prison but the museum authorities have now converted it as a museum extension. The Lamu Museum is on the waterfront, occupying an attractive house in the Indian style; it was once the home and office of colonial district commissioners. Before that, it had housed Her Brittanic Majesty's Consul, one Captain Jack Haggard, brother of the more celebrated Rider Haggard, the novelist.

Mosques are numerous, over 40 of them, although few have any significant architectural merit. In the absence of minarets, they are located either by the loudspeakers calling worshippers to prayer, or a little while after that by the shoes and sandals left on the threshold. The principal mosque is the Riyadha, built in 1901 and a trifle gaudy, which occupies a commanding site in the west, just outside the stone town. Next to the mosque is a college of Islamic learning. A translation of the Arabic inscription above its doors reads:

> This is a meadow of learning;
> These are streams flowing that dwellers here may drink their sweetness,
> He who abides here gains his final goal and those who visit get their wishes too.

Maulidi, the celebration of the Prophet's birthday, is a major event in Lamu and attracts pilgrims not only from Kenya but from all of East Africa, and farther afield too. The religious ceremonies take place in the square in front of the Riyadha and as night falls no visitor, Muslim or non-Muslim, can fail to be moved by the fervour of the occasion. *Maulidi* is also an occasion for dances and singing to be publicly

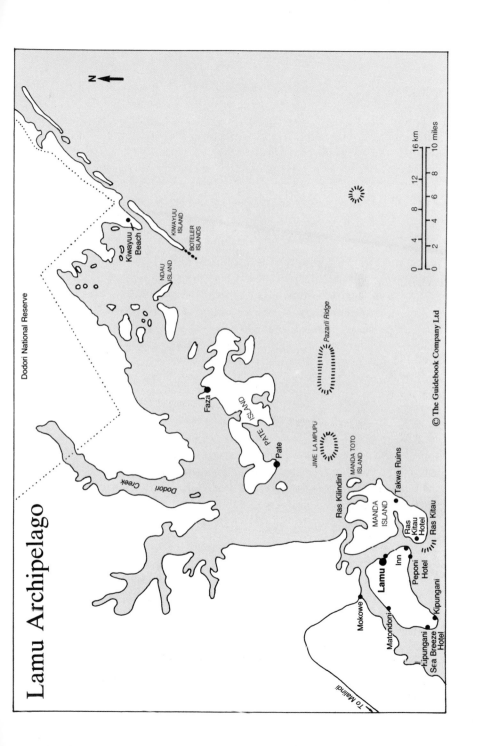

Lamu Archipelago

Dodori National Reserve

N

Kiwayuu Beach

KIWAYUU ISLAND

BOTELER ISLANDS

NDAU ISLAND

Faza

PATE ISLAND

Pate

Pazarli Ridge

JIME LA MPUPU

Dodori Creek

Ras Kilindini

MANDA TOTO ISLAND

MANDA ISLAND

Takwa Ruins

Ras Kitau Hotel

Ras Kitau

Inn

Peponi Hotel

Lamu

Kipungani

Mokowe

Matondoni

Kipungani Sea Breeze Hotel

To Malindi

© The Guidebook Company Ltd

| 0 | | 4 | | 8 | | 12 | | 16 km |

| 0 | 2 | 4 | 6 | 8 | 10 miles |

Trying It On

Juma was a Swahili from the Coast, or said he was: Swahilis were fashionable, and quite a lot of people who were nothing of the sort appointed themselves as members of this race, with its Arab affinities. He also claimed to be a Muslim, though it was hard to say in what this consisted. We never saw him at his prayers and doubted if he knew the direction of Mecca. His only strict observance was his refusal to eat meat unless the throat of the animal providing it had been cut. So when Robin shot a buck, a knife would materialize in Juma's hand, he would gird his long white knazu round his waist (he wore nothing underneath) and sprint like a flash to the stricken antelope. He was a great meat-lover.

"We are coming now to the country of the cannibals," he said facetiously, and quite untruthfully. "These Kikuyu, they scavenge like hyenas, they will dig up corpses and eat them. Sometimes their women give birth to snakes and lizards. They have never heard of Allah. They eat the intestines of goats and circumcise their women. They——"

"Silence, Juma!" Tilly commanded. She was hot, tired, dusty and in no mood for anatomical gossip, and her understanding of the Swahili tongue was still shaky. Although she had studied it with her usual energy and grasp on the voyage out, her phrase-book, acquired from the Society for the Propagation of the Gospel, had not always suggested sentences most helpful to intending settlers. "The idle slaves are scratching themselves". . . "Six drunken Europeans have killed the cook". . . turning these over in her mind, on top of the oxcart in the sun, she doubted if their recital, even in the best Swahili, would impress Juma favourably.

Elspeth Huxley, The Flame Trees of Thika

performed. The celebrations last several days, and despite the problems created by crowds and the strain on the town's fragile infrastructure, it is a time not to be missed. As the date of the birthday varies from year to year, anyone planning to visit Lamu during *Maulidi* should check the date well in advance (the Lamu Museum authorities are always willing to help).

The museum is a gem, housing a collection of Swahili artefacts, jewellery and crafts quite unequalled elsewhere. The two most important items in the museum's collection are the *siwa*, ritual horns from Pate and Lamu. The former, made in 1688 of intricately carved ivory, is over two metres (seven feet) long. These horns are totally unique and when one was taken to London for an exhibition no insurer was able to value it, as no other example existed with which to compare it. The museum also operates a small Swahili house some distance away, which has been set up as representative of the heyday of Lamu in the early part of the 19th century.

When you wander through the streets of Lamu, the coral rag houses appear both formidable and similar. They evolved that way because frequent raids from neighbouring city-states made any display of wealth quite foolish. A great way to find out more about the town and its lifestyle is to rent a house within the town. Many such houses have been bought by foreigners and modernized, hopefully discreetly, and can be rented. If that does not appeal, then stay at Petley's Inn, a 19th-century house converted sympathetically, which overlooks the harbour. Unless you are an early riser it tends to be noisy around dawn, with the shouts and cries of boatmen seeking passengers for their journeys to the outer islands or to the mainland.

There are very many lodging houses in the town, where you share a room or dormitory, and which attract the younger visitors, both for their informality and for their low cost.

The beach begins at **Shela**, a 45-minute walk from the town (or 15 minutes in a motorized boat). Once a sleepy Swahili hamlet, it has been discovered by wealthy Europeans and turned into a miniature St Tropez. It has a delightful 'Friday mosque', the only mosque on the island with a minaret. Just under the minaret and at the very beginning of the beach is Peponi Hotel, small, elegant and lovingly managed. Here you can windsurf, fish, either inshore or deep-sea, or just relax and relish the wonderful beach and the exquisite seafood.

Exploring the archipelago requires some determination, a lot of patience and a good deal of planning. Discuss your wishes with a local boat owner. He will help you with an itinerary that takes account of time and tide and the cost. Probably you have to be prepared to sleep out under the stars. In that event, the most important piece of luggage is a mosquito net. Don't be misled into thinking that a sailing *dhow* is the way to travel. Much nicer, of course, than the smelly diesel inboards, but much slower too, and extremely likely to get out of gear with the tides. You need a lot of time to travel the islands this way.

Pate is well worth a visit, an old town surrounded by tobacco gardens and fallen cannon. Nowadays you can walk from Pate town to **Siyu**, which is not much larger than a village but where a magnificent fort, recently restored, guards nothing but history. With more time you should go on to **Kiwaiyuu**. This island sports the most marvellous beach, where you will be quite alone. Five kilometres of brilliant soft sand backed by dunes, it must rank as one of the last undiscovered glimpses of paradise.

On the mainland near the island is a hostelry that defies classification. The simple palm cabins belie the luxury of the service and the food. This is a place where people weary of the modern trappings of the rich find relaxation without sacrifice. The place is called **Kiwayuu**. There is a somewhat similar establishment on a small island north of Manda Island, called Blue Safaris, which caters in the same luxuriously primitive way for game-fishermen and scuba-diver enthusiasts.

A baobab (Adansonia digitata) *and sacred ibis* (Threskiornis Aethiopicus)*, Kilifi*

A Trove of Ruins

Kenya, and particularly its coastline, is rich in archeological treasures. The earliest date back to the first Islamic colonization in the tenth century, but there were certainly trading expeditions to the coast of what is now Kenya five centuries earlier.

Along the coast, 31 sites containing the standing ruins of at least 53 mosques have been identified—the richest inventory along the whole of the East African littoral.

The Arab or Islamic 'colonies' were soon integrated with the indigenous population. Each of the settlements maintained its internal independence and looked seawards for its prosperity as a trading entrepôt. In consequence, these little 'city-states' were especially dependent on the goodwill and co-operation of the inhabitants of the hinterland, without which their permanence would always be in question. The arrival of the Portuguese at the beginning of the 16th century did much to disrupt the trade and the prosperity of the city-states, except for **Malindi**, whose sultan established and maintained a friendship with the Portuguese from the arrival of Vasco Da Gama in 1498 until the last of the invaders left in the middle of the 18th century (the Cross of Lisbon limestone bearing the arms of Portugal, set up by Da Gama in 1499, even now remains intact).

The Portuguese period left very few cultural legacies and had seemingly no impact on the existing culture except for a few words, such as *mesa*, which were absorbed into Swahili. In the last decade of the 16th century, the Portuguese erected the well-known citadel at the entrance to Mombasa harbour, **Fort Jesus**, which stands in good condition to this day. They certainly needed it, with so many enemies around them. The warlike **Galla** from the north pillaged their way to Mombasa in the second half of the 16th century, while **Mirale Beque**, a Turkish emir, made holy war against the Christian settlers along the whole coast of Azania. And as if that were not enough, the Zimba cannibals from the area of the Zambesi reached the gates of Malindi in 1589. By the 1740s the Portuguese had gone, leaving only Fort Jesus and the crops they had brought from the Americas—potatoes, maize(corn), tomatoes, cashews and tobacco.

The Portuguese exodus was followed by a new wave of Arab colonization. Throughout the 18th century Omanis settled in numerous places along the coast, finally transferring their seat of government from Muscat to

Zanzibar in 1832. Of the many archeological sites so far uncovered, the most dramatic is **Gede**, 20 kilometres (13 miles) south of Malindi. Although the first photographs of this Kenyan Angkor Wat were taken in 1884, it was not until 1948 that work on uncovering Gede began. There are two puzzling questions about this place: why was it built so far from the sea, and why was it so hastily abandoned in the 16th century? Any answers must be conjecture. The outer wall of Gede encloses about 18 hectares (45 acres). An informed guess would put the former population at between 2,000 and 2,500. The mosques and wells in the more distant parts of the city suggest a scattered population, rather than a close-knit community around the palace. This imposing building with its great doorway contains a large, sunken courtyard where the sultan held audience.

The Lamu archipelago contains much of archeological interest. Firstly the town of Lamu itself, with its labyrinthine streets and forbidding coral rag houses so clearly unchanged in centuries, transports the observer to the times of the sultans and the Omani invaders. North of Lamu lie the islands of **Manda** and Pate. On the former there are three sites, **Kitau**, **Manda** and **Takwa**. Manda's remains can be traced back to the ninth century, but a more interesting site to visit is **Takwa**, which lies at the top of a creek, and is easily reached by sailing *dhow* from Lamu town. The remains of a four-hectare (ten-acre) settlement are well preserved—it is thought that Takwa may have been some sort of religious retreat. The Great Mosque and an important pillar tomb (which is still visited twice yearly by Lamu people who go there to pray for rain) are in exceptional condition. **Pate** town on Pate Island was founded, according to the *Pate Chronicle,* by Omani refugees in the eighth century but archeological evidence puts the date much later. If the *Pate Chronicle* is to be believed, Pate was the most powerful of the sultanates in the first half of the 14th century:

In the year of the Hejira 732 (AD 1331), Sultan Omar bin Mohamed took the throne. He made war on the Lamu people until they sued for peace and took allegiance. The sultan's power increased; he fought a number of Swahili towns, Ozi [Kau], Malindi, Kiwaiyuu, Kitau, Miya, Imithi, Watamu until he came to Kilwa [in present-day Tanzania]. He ruled all the cities from Pate to Kilwa and in every city he put his representative to judge. On the eastern side he ruled as far as Washiekh [beyond Mogadishu in Somalia].

Later, the builders in Pate were to create some of the most elaborate and intriguing houses along the whole of the coast and artisans worked fine jewellery of gold and silver, superb furniture and hand-illuminated Korans in the Ki-Amu dialect. Farther to the north is the ruined town of **Shanga**, where excavations have recently begun, and it is now believed to be the oldest and most sophisticated of the early settlements. Finds of coins minted in Shanga tell of its importance.

Visitors to Kenya who come for the sunshine and the beaches will generally stay not far from Mombasa. That city's Old Town (mostly 19th century) and Fort Jesus, now a museum, are obvious places of interest, but just a little farther away, on the north bank of Mtwapa Creek, is *Jumba la Mtwana,* 'the slavemaster's house'. It is a delightful place, with two mosques, one sliding imperceptibly into the ocean. For visitors staying on the South Coast, there is a perfect little mosque at **Kongo**, a little to the north of Golden Beach Hotel. This 15th-century building with its barrel-vaulted roof is still in use. Some people look at these archeological treasures and see only heaps of stones. For others, they represent ten centuries of history.

Fort Jesus, Mombasa, 1928

Kenya For The Adventurous

In Kenya it is a little difficult to tell what is on and what is off the beaten track. You might well be forgiven for thinking that some of the major roads are unbeaten tracks. The road from Kilaguni in Tsavo to Amboseli National Park, for instance, is sometimes not really much more than giant potholes joined one to another by dust pits. So in this chapter we are not so much talking of the track itself but rather the destination. Quite surprisingly, some parts of Kenya that are relatively easy to access are virtually unknown, except to the people who live there. Take for instance **Trans Nzoia**. The Nzoia is a reasonably large river that starts in the **Cherangani Hills**, runs roughly westward from there to the southern foothills of Mount Elgon and thence southwesterly to reach Lake Victoria at Port Victoria. Crossing the Nzoia seems al-

View from Island Camp, Lake Baringo (above);
Bathing in Lake Turkana (left)

most like entering another country, yet its main town, **Kitale**, is
only 400 kilometres (250 miles) from Nairobi. Kitale came into
existence with the slave trade from Uganda. In the grounds of the
Kitale Club is a circle of stones that is said to have once had an iron
ring in the centre to which slaves were fastened. Marjorie Pharazyn,
describing her experiences in the early 1920s, wrote:

> A trip to Nairobi was a major enterprise. By mule cart to Eldoret, then
> by trotting ox-cart service we travelled through the dark night,
> stopping every ten miles to change oxen and drivers, to Londiani,
> where we transferred to the Uganda Railway. The old-fashioned
> carriages were roomy and one took ones bedding if one wanted any.
> When the train stopped at mealtimes all the passengers got out for
> delightful meals served in the station dining room of fresh eggs, tea,
> bread and butter and jam, and much chat with one's fellow travellers.

Travelling to **Eldoret** and Kitale nowadays is not much of an
effort; there is a tarmac road all the way from Nairobi, yet it seems
only to be used by the people who live in Trans Nzoia. There are
two areas in Trans Nzoia that will interest the curious and those
who delight in spectacular scenery. These are the **Mount Elgon**
area, especially the **Mount Elgon National Park** and **Saiwa Swamp
National Park**, Kenya's smallest. The route from Nairobi would
(preferably) take you via Lake Nakuru, already described on p 77,

to **Lake Baringo**.

Lake Baringo is a freshwater lake, so you can swim in it or water ski, despite the hippo and the crocodile—the latter are said to be not interested in humans and the hippo is purely vegetarian. The placid lake has the serenity of a Scottish loch, overlooked in the east by the looming **Marmanet Escarpment**. Birders make a point of going to Baringo for its profusion of birds; **Lake Baringo Club**, on the western lakeshore near Kampi ya Samaki, employs a resident ornithologist to introduce and initiate. **Island Camp** on a small island in the lake is tented and not only enjoys the mystique that all islands have but has a fine reputation for caring hospitality. Just before you reach Lake Baringo you pass the small trading centre of Marigat. There are two directions to go from here. One is a short haul to **Lake Bogoria**, where flamingos are often more numerous than in the more celebrated Lake Nakuru. There are also some awesome hot springs belching boiling water and sulphur-like miniature volcanoes. A plus for visiting Lake Bogoria is that there is a very good chance of seeing greater kudu, the only place in the country where they can be found without a special search being mounted. The other destination from Marigat, and the one we set out to travel, is the climb west to **Kabarnet**. A new highway rises through spectacular scenery up the western wall of the Rift Valley to reach Kabarnet, the Baringo District headquarters, after 40 kilometres (25 miles). There is nothing to detain you at Kabarnet, although there is a small pleasant hotel, and so you plunge on, almost literally, descending into the **Kerio Valley**. This must be one of the most dramatic roads in the country, with breathtaking views if you can take your eyes off the hairpin bends. Moreover, the recently constructed road is wide and smooth. Stop near the bridge across the Kerio to see the river plunge through a rock chasm. An equally fine road, with splendid views, climbs the western wall with spider-like determination. It is hard to comprehend that barely 30 years ago no road of any sort existed and mail was carried by runner from the district headquarters on either side and exchanged (if the runners had not been resorting to too much of the local brew) at the footbridge over the Kerio. The flat valley floor is well farmed, but note the profusion of leopard orchids, *Anselia gigantea*, which festoon almost every tree. There is a fluorspar mine in the valley. When you reach the top of the escarpment, you are at **Iten**, where St Patrick's High School turns out generation after generation of fine Kenyan distance runners.

If you are making for Mount Elgon you will pass through Eldoret and on to Kitale. From Kitale you look for the Endebess road (not very difficult as the town is quite small), then branch left off that road to the well-signposted park and the **Mount Elgon Lodge**. In the absence of any other accommodation, this lodge will have to do, for what it lacks in facilities and creature comforts is made up for by very well-intentioned staff.

You need a four-wheel-drive vehicle to travel in the park, and if wet (which it

The first train to leave Kilindi at the opening of the Kilindi Station, 1901

often is) you need one to reach the lodge. The chief attraction of the park is its caves. There are many around the foothills of the mountain, certainly more than 50, but two major ones are easily accessible soon after entering through the **Chorlim Gate**, just a kilometre or two from the lodge. The better known of the two, **Kitum**, has been made famous by the visiting elephants who come to dig minerals deep inside the cave. Ian Redmond, a biologist who has made a long-term study of the Elgon elephants, thinks that the caves were dug, or at least enlarged, by these nocturnal visits over many centuries. However, early British settlers in the district said they found Masai living in several of the caves with their livestock and that the caves had evidence (chisel- and axe-marks) of having been man-made. It is quite easy to observe the marks made by tusks, so the caves were probably formed by a combination of the two. In the 1980s, the Elgon elephants took a hammering from poachers (mainly Ugandan—the border bisects the mountain). One elephant was shot and killed at the mouth of Kitum Cave. Poaching is well under control now, and the elephants have started to make their almost nightly visits to the caves. The other principal cave is **Makingeny**, very near to Kitum. As in all Kenyan national parks, visitors are not allowed to leave their vehicles but in Elgon you are allowed to walk the short distance, less than a kilometre, to the caves.

Besides visiting the caves, you can drive through the beautiful indigenous forest, well-populated by elephant and buffalo. At around 3,000 metres (10,000 feet) you reach the moorlands, where for much of the year everlasting flowers carpet the land to the horizon. From the end of the car track it is a two-hour walk to the crater of Mount Elgon and the peaks within it. These peaks are the remnants of the volcanic 'plug', which once soared another 1,000 metres (3,300 feet) higher than the present summit. The tallest of the peaks, **Wagagai**, is 4,321 metres (14,178 feet) and is in Uganda, but several on the Kenya side are only a few metres lower. Elgon does not attract mountaineers as it provides no worthwhile climbing, offering instead hill walking with long views and exciting moorland scenery. At this altitude it can be quite cold, so be well provided with clothing to shed when necessary, and bear in mind that snow and ice can make conditions quite unpleasant, especially in the rainy months of April, May, August and September. The peaks are shaped somewhat like breasts, which is the translation of the Maa expression *Ol Doinyo Ilgoon*, hence the anglicized name.

Saiwa Swamp National Park is about 40 kilometres (24 miles) from Kitale off the main highway to Kapenguria. A Kenya Wildlife Services signboard points right after 28 kilometres (18 miles); thereafter, a maze-like route through smallholdings brings you to the gate. You will have come all this way to see the sitatunga, a semi-aquatic antelope whose elongated feet enable it to walk on otherwise treacherous mud and that prefers to graze almost immersed in water. Happily, the sitatunga is easily seen, especially from the Wendy houses that are perched somewhat precariously in trees overlooking the swamp. There is something bizarre about watching an antelope enjoying this apparently unnatural habitat. In the trees around the swamp are some of Kenya's prettiest birds, among them several species of turaco. There are also plenty of monkeys, including De Brazza's, which you will almost certainly not see on a standard game-park tour. Colobus monkeys are also plentiful. Perhaps the greatest delight at Saiwa, however, is being able to walk everywhere; there are no roads and so no vehicles. Being alone, on foot, in an animal sanctuary is a great experience.

After Saiwa you can extend your western Kenya trip to the **Cherangani Hills**. Ten of the 15 peaks within the range exceed 3,075 metres (10,000 feet) and the highest, **Kamelogonis,** is 3,550 metres (11,540 feet). The hills are heavily forested, although sadly much of the land has now been cleared for farming. At the higher levels, giant groundsels, heathers and lobelia occur in some profusion. The bongo antelope, the most elusive of all Kenya's animals, occurs here and you may encounter one on a hill-walking expedition. Although too far away to be on Kenya's fishing map, there is passable trout fishing in the Marun River high in the hills (but easily reached, where the river crosses the main road that traverses the Cheranganis). This road starts at **Kapenguria**, an untidy, overgrown village, famous as the location of the trial of Mzee

Setting off for safari, Government Road, Nairobi, 1907

Modern camel safari

Jomo Kenyatta.

If you are exploring western Kenya you will not want to return to Nairobi the way you came, so a visit to the **Kakamega Forest** is a good idea. In fact, for the explorer it is a must, since in Kenya it is unique. The forest is a small remnant of the rain forest that once covered all of central Africa from Kakamega westward to the Atlantic Ocean. Climatic changes and the development of agriculture in Uganda and Kenya have caused the rain forest to retreat to eastern Zaire, leaving Kakamega as a show-piece of West African flora and fauna. It is worth going all the way to the Kakamega Forest to see the great blue turaco, the largest and definitely the most beautiful of a dazzling family. What R B Woosnam has described as the finest birdsong heard in Africa gives the joyful greenbul its lovely name. This golden-green bird is common in the forest. Bird enthusiasts will want to see the blue-headed bee-eater, found only in the Kakamega Forest. There are other winged delights in the form of butterflies of great variety and abundance. It is not difficult to find well over a hundred species in a day or two, among them the huge swallowtails. The western emperor swallowtail, *Papilio Lormieri*, with a wingspan of 13 centimetres (five inches), is quite common.

Another source of interest in the forest are the monkeys. Colobus, of course, but also the much rarer red-tailed monkey, much the same size as the very common vervet but with a conspicuous white face. The blue monkey, closely related to Sykes's, is easy to see because it is gregarious and diurnal. You may also be lucky enough to see—by torchlight—the Potto, a thickset, short-tailed primate, which in Kenya is confined to the Kakamega Forest. Mention should also be made of the largest bat found on the African mainland, the hammer-headed fruit bat, which must rank among God's less attactive creations—as its scientific name, *Hypsignathus monstrosus*, suggests. You are more likely to see huge colonies of the straw-coloured fruit bat that appear in clouds at dusk. There is comfortable accommodation in nearby Kakamega town (at the Golf Hotel), and there is an interesting self-catering tree lodge within the forest.

The classic traveller's destination is **Lake Turkana**, the Jade Sea. A Hungarian count, Samuel Teleki von Szek, and his companion, Lieutenant Ludwig von Hohnel, were the first Europeans to reach the lake, on 5 March 1888. Von Hohnel wrote '..an entirely new world was spread out before our astonished eyes. The void down in the depths beneath became filled as if by magic with picturesque mountains and rugged slopes, with a medley of ravines and valleys which appeared to be closing up from every side to form a fitting frame for the dark-blue gleaming surface of the lake stretching away beyond as far as the eye could reach.' They named the lake Rudolf in honour of their patron, Prince Rudolf of Austria, though it was renamed in 1975. The journey from Zanzibar on foot had taken 13 months.

Your journey from Nairobi, by Land-Rover, will take less than two days. The route to the eastern shore is via Nyahururu and Maralal, to the western shore via Eldoret, Kitale, Kapenguria and Lodwar. The eastern route is preferable for reasons both of distance and scenery. Stop for a while at Nyahururu to marvel at the falls named by and after another intrepid explorer, Joseph Thomson, who arrived there in October 1883. 'On reaching them, I was impressed mightily by the stupendous thundering of the waters which in magnificent mass plunged down several hundred feet without a break into a fearful gloomy gorge.' Getting a glimpse of this 'magnificent mass' falling 75 metres (243 feet) is unfortunately more difficult today because the inevitable curio-sellers have commandeered the best vantage points.

The place for a nightstop is **Maralal**, the headquarters of Samburu District, probably in the delightful little lodge built of local mountain cedar. The lodge's lounge and dining room overlook a waterhole, offering views almost all day of zebra, impala, warthog and eland. In the evening, when the stage is floodlit, buffalo take their turn in this seemingly endless pageant. The tiny wildlife sanctuary in which the lodge stands has practically no legal protection but is adequately endowed with smaller animals in a setting as tranquil and pretty as any found in the larger parks. The sprawling and untidy township merits a visit, if only to contrast the finery of the Samburu and Turkana folk who strut the streets, with the drabness of their urban surroundings. There is usually petrol available in town, but the wise driver will be carrying plenty in any case, since no supplies exist after Maralal.

Soon after leaving Maralal, the road passes through a cedar forest; its condition serves notice that the next 250 kilometres (156 miles) will be a vehicle- and body-shattering experience. It is advisable to set out for the lake at the first hint of light to allow time for a deviation to enjoy a spectacular view of the Great Rift Valley at a place that Europeans call **Losiolo**, but which the locals refer to as *N'gerem*. The track that heads west to the rift leaves the 'main' road about 15 kilometres (ten miles) from Maralal, and is found opposite a small plantation forest. Stay on this track until you can go no farther, since it stops at the escarpment, where there is a 500 metre (1,600 feet) drop to the valley floor. The view is absolutely stunning. Return to the main road and head once again for the lake. As you descend from the forests the route becomes hot and dusty and even the tiny settlements at Merti and Baragoi seem like oases. On the way to Baragoi you may be able to spot greater kudu, for this is one of the few places where they are regularly seen. At **South Horr**, about 140 kilometres (88 miles) from Maralal, there is indeed an oasis. You may want to rest here by a sparkling stream, for the journey, not counting the digression to the escarpment, will have taken some five hours. You might even wish to stay the night; if so, there is a fine little cabin camp nearby at **Karungu**. The area is spectacular, with forested mountains on either side. If you are keen to see the lake from here (and extremely fit) you can scale **Mount Nyiru**, and from its peak at 2,770 metres (9,000 feet) there are

THE FLYING DOCTORS

In 1957, three doctors, among them the late Sir Michael Wood, discussed the notion that aviation could revolutionize the spread and quality of modern medicine in Africa. In addition to the minute amount of money available for health services, radio could bring widespread benefits; specialist services could reach the remotest corner of the land and seriously sick patients could be transferred to distant hospitals. The discussion led to the establishment of the Flying Doctor Service, the first operation of the African Medical and Research Foundation (AMREF), which now runs numerous medical projects throughout eastern Africa.

Today, there are over 120 radio stations linked to the headquarters of the Flying Doctors at Wilson airport, Nairobi. Often the radio is the only means of fast communication in remote areas and medical stations rely on it to obtain advice on complicated cases, to send requests for drugs and to arrange emergency evacuations or medical transfers. At Wilson airport, the radios are manned around the clock by qualified medical staff who can attend to these requests. In the case of emergency evacuation, the flight nurses are all trained in emergency medicine and in-flight care of the patient. On arrival, the Flying Doctors' own ambulance is waiting and casualty staff and specialists who have been alerted by radio are on hand.

While emergency work is the best known aspect of the Flying Doctor Service, other activities now include plastic surgery on leprosy patients; a malaria project; research into tsetse flies and into hydatid disease; a disaster unit; and the Medicine by Air programme currently run by the redoubtable Dr Anne Spoerry. Funding for the Flying Doctors is a constant and continuing problem. In 1971, Mrs Maddie de Mott and Sir Michael Wood set up the Flying Doctors' Society to assist in providing finance. The society has grown into a considerable organization, raising money by membership subscriptions, donations, and through their shop at AMREF's building at Wilson airport. A special tourist membership is available at a cost of US$20 and is valid for one month; some tour operators automatically include this membership in the price of their tours. While most visitors will not need the services of the Flying Doctors when on safari, and can therefore regard their membership fee as a donation, it is comforting to know that in the event of serious illness or an accident, free emergency treatment and air transport to the nearest suitable medical facility will be handled swiftly and professionally.

Flying doctors over the Great Rift Valley

splendid views over Teleki's volcano to the lake beyond. The forests of Mount Nyiru harbour elephant and buffalo, so you will be wise to take a local guide and exercise special caution.

Soon after leaving the Horr Valley the road deteriorates as the landscape becomes more arid and boulder-strewn. At this stage you may be wondering why you ever made the journey—but such unworthy thoughts will be dispelled at the first sight of the great lake. It will be another hour before you reach the water. The Jade Sea is nearly 260 kilometres (160 miles) in length and 56 kilometres (35 miles) at its widest point. The total area is about 6,400 square kilometres (2,470 square miles).

Lake Turkana was not always like this. Only 400 years ago you would have seen its shimmering waters from your lookout at Losiolo, as the lake then reached almost to Lake Baringo. Its diminution is mainly due to climatic changes, although volcanic activity must also have played a part. In Teleki's day there were plenty of elephants along the lake, indicating much more vegetation than is now found. Today there are no elephants. A more dramatic reminder of the past is the petrified forest near **Allia Bay**, where the size of the fossilized tree trunks provides evidence of luxuriant vegetation impossible to imagine in today's scorched and desolate landscape. There is still some sort of vegetation today, although in most places it is hard to find, but there is enough in **Sibiloi National Park** to support some wildlife, including lion, cheetah and hyena, as well as zebra, Grant's gazelle and the tiang, a race of the more familiar topi. The park was really gazetted to protect the hominid finds of Richard Leakey's fossil hunting team, which has scoured the area since 1968 and continues to do so. Some of these finds are on show at the makeshift museum situated at **Koobi Fora**, the fossil hunters' headquarters. There is also some accommodation that can be rented by giving prior notice to the National Museum in Nairobi.

There are motorable tracks from **Loiyangalani**, the only trading post on the east side of the lake, to Sibiloi and Koobi Fora; and there is an airstrip at the latter. There is also a strip at Loiyangalani, serving the **Oasis Lodge**—a haven if ever there was one. It is also the destination of fishermen who come to land the enormous Nile perch that abound in Lake Turkana and can reach 100 kilograms (220 pounds). The lodge keeps a flotilla of boats for fishing and exploration. The lake has the world's largest population of Nile crocodile (one estimate puts the number at 12,000) but these are best seen in the northern parts and on **Central Island** (itself a national park), where they breed. The breeding season is around October and November, and the eggs are laid a month later. Incubation takes about three months, so the young emerge in February and March.

Central Island is a short boat trip from **Lake Turkana Fishing Lodge**, a comfortable collection of wooden buildings set on a promontory 65 kilometres (40 miles) northeast of **Lodwar**, on the western side of the lake. Not very many years ago this promontory almost encircled Ferguson's Gulf and had to be reached by boat from the roadhead. Today the gulf is totally dry, visible evidence of the still receding waters of the lake. The journey to the lake on the western side is relatively easy, for there is tarmac all the way. Once again, it is possible to hire fishing boats at the lodge and to use their boats for expeditions to Central Island, and possibly Koobi Fora. However, an easier way to Koobi Fora is by air, since it is possible to charter the Air Kenya plane that arrives at Ferguson's Gulf on a scheduled service. Birdwatching in the Ferguson's Gulf area is rewarding (as it is in other parts of the lake) and during the northern hemisphere's winter months the shallow waters host thousands of migrant waders and waterfowl. There are also resident species in huge numbers, particularly pelicans, flamingos, ibises and spoonbills.

Because of the heat and the fierce winds not many people stay long at the lake. If you have driven in a four-wheel-drive to the eastern side, and if you feel like tackling more explorer country, you will head for **Marsabit** across the **Chalbi Desert**. In any event, Marsabit is another of the destinations that the intrepid traveller should visit. Leaving Loiyangalani, head north for North Horr, which is just as desolate as its name suggests. It is advisable to be in a party of at least two vehicles and certainly you should take plenty of food and water in case of an enforced stay. The road marked on the C77 map scarcely exists, and drivers generally follow the tracks that seem most used. There is a rather lonely lodge at Marsabit too.

North Horr lies in the lee of a considerable hill called Dabandabli, so aim for this. From North Horr you head southeast to Maikona, which is nothing more than a mission station and the odd *duka*. This section takes you across the Chalbi Desert, once a huge lake and now occasionally so if there has been heavy rain. The route is still quite indistinct but the general direction is easy to follow, since the desert lies between two ranges of hills—the **Huri Hills** to the northeast, which stretch to Ethiopia, and an unnamed range that reaches 1,080 metres (3,520 feet) to the southwest. The journey is enlivened by the nomads who are often found with large herds of their disdainful camels.The herdsmen are likely to be Rendille in the west, and Boran or Gabbra to the east.These camels represent a bank balance, and it is sobering to think that quite serious wealth has been accrued in such hostile conditions. But material possessions scarcely exist and are not even sought after. The nomads' domestic animals and the water and vegetation required to sustain them seem to be all that are needed. No other form of lifestyle is possible in these conditions. The journey from Loiyangalani to Marsabit covers about 250 kilometres (156 miles). On the way you will have learned much about the climate, the tenacious vegetation, and the serenity and strength of the local people. When you see Marsabit mountain from a distance you will wonder how such dense forest can grow in the middle of a desert. It certainly isn't due to rain, as only 250–500 millimetres (10–20 inches) falls in a good year. It is actually cloud forest, for the mountain is shrouded in mist most days until late morning. The town of Marsabit lies at the forest edge on the crown of the mountain; it is the headquarters of a district that happens to be the largest in the country. Trade is mostly in livestock but its attraction, if that is the right word, is the amazing miscellany of country folk whose clothes and hairstyles reflect a vivid variety of cultures. In addition to the Rendille, Gabbra and Boran whom you may have met on the way, there are Ethiopians, Somalis and numerous Samburu.

Marsabit National Park is very close to the town. This is the park of great elephants. Ahamed, the animal whose fibreglass replica now guards the entrance to the National Museum in Nairobi, was once king here and his successor, Mohammed, carries tusks each of which are said to exceed 45 kilograms (100 pounds). Within the park are three crater lakes, *Gof Sokorte Dika, Gof Sokorte Guda* and *Gof Bongole*. Only the second of these has an English name—**Lake Paradise**—given by the celebrated American film-makers, Martin and Osa Johnson, in the 1920s. The dense forest makes game viewing difficult, except when animals come to the craters to drink. There are many greater kudu on the mountain, and unless your visit is a fleeting one, it should be possible to see these. Lion, leopard, buffalo and the rarer striped hyena can also be found. Before leaving the idyllic beauty of the forest and heading south to what we call civilization, you should look at one or two of the other *gofs* outside the park. Just three kilometres (one and a half miles) from the town is *Gof Redo*, a considerable crater about 200 metres (650 feet) deep and filled with *Euphorbia candelabrum*. Redo is just one of many craters that pit the area, as if someone in space had used the mountain for target practice. On leaving Marsabit town on the road to Isiolo you pass the famous 'singing wells' at **Ulanula**. The wells do not of course sing, but the Boran who draw water there for their cattle do. Driving along the corrugated road back to the tarmac at Isiolo is uncomfortable but otherwise uneventful.

The Less Visited National Parks and Reserves

The following 31 parks and reserves are described only briefly. An asterisk beside some names indicates that these sanctuaries are also mentioned elsewhere in this book.

Aberdare National Park

The whole of the Aberdare range above the 3,050-metre (10,000-feet) contour is within the park, together with a projection that plunges to the forest edge on the eastern side of the park, at around 1,830 metres (6,000 feet). Both **Treetops** and the **Ark**, two famous tree hotels, are in this area, known locally as 'The Salient'. These tree hotels both offer surprisingly comfortable accommodation from which to observe game at night, by floodlights. There is a good road that traverses the park from east to west, but it is not advisable to use it except in a four-wheel-drive vehicle. Even in January and February, when the weather is reliably dry, there are occasions on which a sudden storm has stranded visitors. Within the forest are elephant, rhino, buffalo and giant forest hog, and although these are hard to spot because of the nature of the forest, it is quite possible to see all four on a drive across the mountain. You will almost certainly see colobus monkeys and bushbuck, and you may also see leopard and lion. Whether the mountain lions are a distinct breed is still controversial, but the lions seen in the Aberdare do seem to retain their juvenile spots throughout their lives. Bongo, the rarest of East Africa's antelopes, live high in the forest, often in the bamboo, but are seldom sighted. Probably the best chance of seeing this splendid animal is at the Ark, although that is far from guaranteed. Even without the game, the moorlands and the high plateau of the park are superb scenic areas. There are several strikingly beautiful waterfalls plunging into the dense forest, which can be observed from prepared viewpoints (you are permitted to wander from your car for a limited distance). The flora is stunning, and for those unable to undertake the strenuous walking required to attain the high reaches of other East African mountains, this may be the only chance to see some of the giant heather, lobelias and groundsels, which turn this park into a fairyland. The main peak of the Aberdare range, **Satima**, reaches a height of just under 4,000 metres (13,120 feet).

Arawale National Reserve

Arawale was established to preserve the Hunter's hartebeest, a relict antelope much more like an impala than the common hartebeest or kongoni. The species is found in a very small part of Kenya and in adjacent Somalia, although there are huge tracts elsewhere in Kenya where a similar habitat exists even if Hunter's hartebeest does not. Arawale is an area of dry, arid bush, is hot and inhospitable, and is really only for the very adventurous and very curious. But it is relatively easy of access, for the Garissa–Ijara–Lamu road passes along its northern boundary. There is no accommodation for visitors.

Bisanadi National Reserve

This reserve protects the eastern flank of Meru National Park, from which it is separated by the Murera and Rojewero rivers. The Bisanadi river is the eastern boundary of the reserve. It is accessible from Meru by a number of small tracks, but is not recommended for a visit at present because of insecurity in the area.

Boni National Reserve

Boni has a boundary both with Somalia and with the Dodori National Reserve. It is difficult to get to and there is no accommodation. Game is plentiful and the coastal-type flora interesting, but like Bisanadi, it has a security problem at present and must therefore be considered a resource more for the future than the present.

Central Island National Park *

A small island in the middle part of Lake Turkana established to protect the breeding areas of the Nile crocodile. A visit to this fascinating place can easily be arranged by the Lake Turkana Fishing Lodge at Ferguson's Gulf. The island is almost entirely occupied by three extinct volcanoes, in whose craters are the slimy green lakes in which the breeding crocodiles live. Their eggs hatch around April and May.

Central Island,
Lake Turkana

Dodori National Reserve

Although this reserve is partly contiguous with Boni, mentioned above, it is easier to reach. There are roads on either side of the reserve, one along the coast and entered from Kiwaiyuu (where there is a delightful get-away-from-it-all hostelry), and the other from Mangai, reached via the Garissa–Ijara road or from Lamu via Hindi and Bodhei. Just north of Kiwaiyuu, only the beach separates the wildlife reserve from the Kiungo Marine Reserve, a combination that must be unique. Dodori has good game possibilities. Lion and elephant are present, and thousands of topi. The reserve is dotted with small lakes in which water birds congregate and where game comes to drink. The Dodori River flows through the reserve into Dodori Creek, where it is possible to scuba-dive among the dugong, which are prevalent in the area.

Hell's Gate National Park *

This is one of the few parks in Kenya where you can walk, and in safety. It is a spectacular area, wild and dramatic. In prehistoric times Lake Naivasha was very much bigger than now and the gorge was its fearsome outlet. The entrance to the gorge is reached by a well-signposted track leading left off Moi South Road through the Sulmac Flower Farm, about five kilometres (three miles) after Lake Naivasha Club. Very near the entrance stands an imposing rock tower, actually the plug of a long since eroded volcano. Called **Fischer's Column** after Dr Gustav Fischer, a German explorer who discovered Hell's Gate, it now hosts a colony of hyrax (and sometimes bees!). There is a fair amount of plains game after Fischer's Column, and birdlife is plentiful. Ornithologists come here to sight the bearded lammergeyer vulture. At the end of the motorable track there are paths leading down the hillside to the hot springs.

Nearby is the geothermal station, the first in Africa, which uses the superheated steam so generously provided by nature. The nearest accommodation is at Lake Naivasha.

Kakamega National Reserve *

A West African-type forest, the only representative of its kind in Kenya. Unbeatable for butterflies and birds, it is also home to insects and flora not found anywhere else in the country. There is comfortable accommodation in Kakamega town, 15 kilometres (nine miles) from the forest.

Kamnarok National Reserve

This small reserve protects the immediate surroundings of tiny Lake Kamnarok and its important birdlife. It lies in the Kerio Valley on the eastern (Baringo) side of the river, about 20 kilometres (13 miles) from the bridge over the Kerio, on the road from Kabarnet to Tambach. There is no accommodation.

Kerio Valley National Reserve

Even smaller than Kamnarok, this reserve protects the celebrated Kerio Gorge, an area of outstanding natural beauty. Accommodation is at Kabarnet, 20 kilometres (13 miles) away.

Kora National Reserve

Larger than the Masai Mara, but with scarcely any game, Kora is best known as the last home of 'Bwana Game', George Adamson, the eccentric husband of the even more eccentric Joy. It lies on the south side of the Tana River and is contiguous with

the southern boundary of Bisanadi. It is an area of dense thornbush with two alleged-
ly motorable tracks. It can be reached by road via Thika and Mwingi but is not recommended except for the fully self-contained walker, and then only when the security situation has been well checked out.

Laikipia National Reserve

The newest of Kenya's wildlife reserves, gazetted in October 1991, and covering 165
square kilometres (64 square miles), it serves to protect a large herd of elephant in a
swampy area.

Lake Bogoria National Reserve *

Lake Bogoria is breathtakingly beautiful and is one of the wonders of the Rift Valley.
The lake sits hard against the sheer eastern wall of the rift, whose cliffs plunge to the
water's edge. Greater kudu roam where the wall is not quite so precipitous, and this is
the best place in Kenya to find these attractive animals. On the western shore are
fearsome fumaroles and hot springs, the steam from which creates a cloud over the
pink swathe of flamingo that habitually decorate the lake. The reserve can be ap-
proached from Lake Baringo, an easy journey of 25 kilometres (16 miles), or by a
rough track from Mogotio, which should only be tackled if you want to immerse
yourself in the healing waters of **Maji Moto** en route!

Longonot National Reserve *

Longonot is a relatively new volcano that overlooks Lake Naivasha. If you want to
climb the mountain, take the track from Longonot station, just off the old Nairobi–
Naivasha Road, and drive until you can't get any farther, about six kilometres (four
miles). You should bring someone with you to look after the car, for the area is open
and can be seen from miles away. The easy climb to the edge of the crater takes about
an hour and a half. Go well provided with shade and drinks, for it can be hot. The
bottom of the crater is forested and you will be able to discern some small steam
vents.

Losai National Reserve

A great expanse of thorn bush and scrub lying to the left of the Isiolo–Marsabit road. It is difficult to understand why it has been declared a reserve.

Marsabit National Reserve *

One of the best kept secrets in Kenya (partly because it is a drive of nearly 600 kilometres [375 miles] from Nairobi), this delightfully scenic forest reserve mantles the crest of a mountain rising sheer from the desert. Cloud produces the dense forest and not much can be seen in the park until well after mid-morning. Huge tusked elephants are plentiful, as well as many other forest species. The reserve contains two beautiful crater lakes, one justly named Lake Paradise, where animals come to drink and where an air of mystery adds charm to an already entrancing scene. There is a simple lodge overlooking one of the crater lakes.

Mount Kenya National Park

This park is a prime attraction for mountaineers. It is possible for the less active to visit part of the park by Land-Rover via the Sirimon track beyond Nanyuki, which reaches nearly 4,000 metres (13,000 feet). On this journey you pass through forest and bamboo and thence to moorland with much scenic variety. Choose a dry time of the year. Climbers must be aware of the dangers of too hasty an ascent, since this combined with physical action can bring on pulmonary oedema. Naro Moru Lodge offers a base for climbing the mountain and also rents out gear and provides porters.

Mwea National Reserve

A little known and little visited reserve only 100 kilometres (60 miles) from Nairobi in the lower part of Embu District. The land surrounding the reserve is heavily cultivated (as are parts of the reserve itself).

Prize List

LIST OF GAME SHOT WITH THE RIFLE DURING THE TRIP

	BY T. R.	BY K. R.
Lion	9	8
Leopard	—	3
Cheetah	—	7
Hyena	5	4
Elephant	8	3
Square-mouthed rhinoceros	5	4
Hook-lipped rhinoceros	8	3
Hippopotamus	7	1
Wart-hog	8	4
Common zebra	15	4
Big or Grévy's zebra	5	5
Giraffe	7	2
Buffalo	6	4
Giant eland	1	2
Common eland	5	2
Bongo	—	2
Kudu	—	2
Situtunga	—	1
Bushbuck		
East African	2	4
Uganda harnessed	1	2
Nile harnessed	3	3
Sable	—	3
Roan	4	5
Oryx	10	3
Wildebeest	5	2
Neumann's hartebeest	—	3

Black rhino, the Aberdares

Coke's hartebeest	10	3
Big Hartebeest		
Jackson's	14	7
Uganda	1	3
Nilotic	8	4
Topi	12	4
Common waterbuck	5	3
Singsing waterbuck	6	6
Common kob	10	6
Vaughn's kob	1	2
White-eared kob	3	2
Saddle-backed lechwe (Mrs. Gray's)	3	1
Bohor reedbuck	10	4
Chanler's buck	3	4
Impalla	7	5
Big gazelle Grant's	5	3
Robertsi	4	6
Notata	8	1
Thomson's gazelle	11	9
Gerenuk	3	2
Klipspringer	1	3
Oribi	18	8
Duiker	3	2
Steinbuck	4	2
Dikdik	1	1
Baboon	—	
Red ground monkey	1	—
Green monkey	—	1
Black and white monkey	5	4
Serval	—	1
Jackal	—	1

Aardwolf	—	1
Rattel	—	1
Porcupine	—	2
Ostrich	2	—
Great bustard	4	3
Lesser bustard	1	1
Kavirondo crane	2	—
Flamingo	—	4
Whale-headed stork	1	1
Marabou	1	1
Saddle-billed stork	1	—
Ibis stork	2	—
Pelican	1	—
Guinea-fowl	5	5
Francolin	1	2
Fish eagle	—	1
Vulture	2	
Crocodile	1	3
Monitor	—	1
Python	3	1
	296	216

Kermit and I kept about a dozen trophies for ourselves; otherwise we shot nothing that was not used either as a museum specimen or for meat— usually for both purposes. We were in hunting grounds practically as good as any that have ever existed; but we did not kill a tenth, nor a hundredth part of what we might have killed had we been willing. The mere size of the bag indicates little as to a man's prowess as a hunter, and almost nothing as to the interest or value of his achievement.

Theodore Roosevelt, African Game Trails, 1910

Nasalot National Reserve

Nasalot lies halfway between Kitale and Lodwar, near the main road, and is dominated by a substantial hill of the same name overlooking the Turkwell Gorge and the new dam, which provides energy for the hydro-electric scheme. There is a limited amount of plains game but otherwise the reserve is not of special interest.

Ndeere Island

A small island in Lake Victoria where there is potentially good fishing and some small mammals but otherwise has yet to be developed.

Ngai Ndethya

This falls into the same category as Mwea and it is hard to know why it is retained as a reserve. It is a sort of buffer zone for Tsavo East National Park, but is widely cultivated and seems hard to justify even for this purpose.

Ol Doinyo Sapuk National Park *

A scenic rather than a wildlife park, which offers a pleasant day trip from Nairobi. Access is via Thika. The forested top of this whale-shaped hill, which was bequeathed to the nation by its one time owner, Sir William Northrup McMillan, is the reserve itself. There are great views on a clear day when both Mount Kenya and Kilimanjaro can easily be seen. There are very few animals, although some buffalo are said to live there. But birdlife is good and the flora is interesting. There are some examples of Afro-Alpine flora, such as the giant lobelia, and there is an indigenous variety of protea (the South African national flower) growing on the stony slopes. Use a four-wheel-drive vehicle if possible.

Rahole National Reserve

This reserve is on the northern bank of the Tana River opposite Kora National Re-

Losiolo: view point over the Great Rift Valley

serve. Its dry thorn scrub is inhospitable and access is difficult, although it can be reached by a rough road from Isiolo via Garba Tula. There are no accommodation facilities. Formerly there were elephants and rhino but poaching in this area has been exceptionally severe and game is scarce. You should also check the security situation with the Garissa police or the district commissioner.

Ruma National Park

This park, formerly called Lambwe Valley, is a delightful spot in an off-circuit location in the South Nyanza District of western Kenya. Access is easy from Homa Bay town. It was originally created to give protection to a herd of roan antelope, a species that has never been numerous in Kenya. Game watching is good, and besides the roan there is also Jackson's hartebeest, a larger, redder species than Coke's, which can be seen in the major parks. The tiny oribi is also easy to see here, plus leopard and cheetah. In fact, the game compares very favourably with the better known parks. The difficulty is that there is no accommodation, and even campers must be totally self-contained, bringing their own water. It is possible to stay at the Homa Bay Hotel, 35 kilometres (22 miles) away, but this is scarcely a tourist-class hotel.

Saiwa Swamp National Park *

Specialized and special, this little park, the smallest in Kenya, hosts the sitatunga antelope, a semi-aquatic species not found elsewhere in the country. It also has Brazza monkeys and some interesting birdlife. No transport is allowed in the park and access to the viewing platforms is on foot. Although a long way to go from Nairobi—about 400 kilometres (250 miles)—it is an easy extension to a visit to Mount Elgon.

Shimba Hills National Reserve*

Rolling hills with patches of rain forest look out over the Indian Ocean. The Shimba Hills are the home of Kenya's few sable antelope populations and also contain other game, large and small. The park is an easy drive from Mombasa or any of the South Coast hotels, and there is a comfortable 'tree house' for overnight stays, where game can be watched at a waterhole by floodlight.

Sibiloi National Park *

This park lies along the northeastern shore of Lake Turkana. The park is dry and arid, but along the shore can be found plenty of oryx, both species of zebra, Peter's gazelle and tiang. All these animals have adapted to feeding in the water, grazing on sub-surface vegetation. Sibiloi also contains a large population of Nile crocodile. The park is famous for its fossil beds, which have yielded much information about early man. It is difficult of access and a four-wheel-drive vehicle is essential.

South Island National Park

This island in the very southern part of Lake Turkana is impossible to reach other than by boat, which has to be hired at Loiyangalani. It contains little of interest and is notable mainly because its rocky shoreline is favoured by large Nile perch. There is a herd of feral goats on the island.

South Kitui National Reserve

This is the most northerly part of Tsavo East National Park and is currently not open to visitors.

South Turkana National Reserve

An isolated area that lies to the east of the main road from Kitale to Lodwar, not far from the Turkwell hydro-electric scheme. It has a small number of plains game but is of little interest to the general visitor.

Tana River Primate National Reserve

The reserve was established to protect the rare red Tana Colobus monkey and the grey mangabey monkey, both of which occur in Kenya only in the riparian gallery forests of the lower Tana. It is a delightful area, with great birdlife and the usual delights of a large, slow-moving river. It is a four-hour journey from Malindi via Garsen, a distance of about 140 kilometres (90 miles).

Some Specialized Activities

The majority of visitors to Kenya go there to see its wealth of wildlife or to luxuriate on its sun-caressed beaches, or perhaps both, but a growing number now go to savour some of its lesser known delights. Kenya offers almost the entire gamut of the Western world's sports and recreational activities as well as more specialized ones such as camel treks or **palaeoanthropology**.

Birdwatchers and photographers are offered unrivalled opportunities in Kenya, and there are specialist safari firms that cater for people seeking species identification only ('twitching' or 'ticking') and for those who, given the right opportunity, wish to study some selected species in detail. Specialist bird photographers should definitely seek the help of a local and competent bird photographer, and such persons are available (see p 18).

Fishing safaris are arranged by most tour operators and by fishing centres at the coast. The best deep-sea fishing is between November and March, although apart from May and June other months can be profitable too. Game fishing is centred on the Lamu archipelago, Malindi and Watamu, Kilifi, Mombasa, Diani Beach and Shimoni. Fishing for Nile perch in Lakes Victoria and Turkana provides great sport and huge catches. Mention has been made (p 176) of two lodges catering for fishermen at Lake Turkana, but there are also two island camps on Lake Victoria.

Climbers will find the main peaks of Mount Kenya a challenge requiring both skill and determination as well as presenting problems of altitude. The Mountain Club of Kenya (PO Box 45741, Nairobi) will be pleased to offer advice and assistance to would-be climbers, and there are several local operators who specialize in this field. Much useful information on Mount Kenya is contained in *Mount Kenya, 1:50,000 Map and Guide* by Andrew Wielochowski and Mark Savage, which is obtainable in Nairobi bookshops or from West Col Productions, Goring, Reading RG8 9AA, England.

Hill walking is also recommended. There are ten mountain ranges exceeding 3,075 metres (10,000 feet) and the enjoyment of walking will be spiced with the excitement of seeing wildlife in almost all these locations. There are specialized tour operators who will organize walking tours to match your energy and budget. It is also possible to go **pony trekking** and **camel trekking** in wildlife country. **Bicycle tours** have just started and interested visitors can research the subject with the operator named on page 18. The warm, limpid waters of the Indian Ocean are a magnet for the **diving** enthusiast and numerous diving schools and clubs along the coast can host scuba-fans. These clubs can supply equipment, which it would be impractical to bring to Kenya for bulk and weight reasons.

Ballooning in the Masai Mara

Golf Tours are becoming increasingly popular and the opening of the new Windsor Golf and Country Club on the outskirts of Nairobi has given a new impetus to the organizers of golfing safaris. The club is an international-class hotel with an adjacent golf course, promoted as the finest in Africa. In addition, there are 13 other courses, which can be categorized as seven = excellent, four = good, and two = average. The weather in Kenya is ideal for golf year-round. You rarely need a sweater and it is never too hot. Most of the courses are scenic, well-maintained and under-used. Up-country courses are generally at a high altitude, from 1,675 metres (5,500 feet) to 2,150 metres (7,000 feet) at Limuru. At these heights you will have the excitement of adding quite a few metres to your shots. No golf carts are available but there are caddies. They take care of everything from looking for your ball in the rough, advising on local rules (such as what to do when the ball falls into a hippo footmark), carrying your golf bag and giving advice, if necessary, on your swing. And you'll probably mix some game viewing with your golf.

In scientific fields, tours are arranged for **archeologists**, or those interested in archeology, which could include guided visits to the **palaeoanthropological** sites. Specialized tours can also be arranged for **industrialists** and **agriculturalists**, whose programmes would normally be combined with wildlife safaris. Almost every interest has its counterpart in Kenya and tours have been planned for groups as diverse as horse-racing fans, lepidopterists, steam railway enthusiasts and rock hounds.

There are some fine convention centres, ranging from the **Kenyatta International Conference Centre** in downtown Nairobi to small halls catering for about 50 participants in several of the game lodges. Seminars will never be the same after you have participated in one at Kilaguni Lodge, where one eye is on the overhead projector and the other on an elephant. Most of the larger Kenyan tour operators have experience in setting up conventions and seminars.

Swahili for the Visitor

It is written and spoken phonetically and there are no dipthongs. For example, the letters 'au' appearing consecutively will be pronounced separately, as in *tofauti*. The vowels are pronounced as follows:

A as in 'hard'
E as in 'hey!'
I as in 'he'
O as in 'hoe'
U as in 'who'
G is always pronounced hard (as in Gordon and not as in George)

There is no Q and X, and C appears only as Ch. Y exists but is never a substitute for I. All true Swahili words end in a vowel, so it follows that syllables do too. The accent is almost always on the last but one syllable.

Some useful words and phrases

Jambo... 'Hello, how do you do?' (note Ja-mbo not Jam-bo). The response is also *Jambo*, although *Nzuri* and *Salama* are used as replies too.

Bwana means 'Mister', although it used to be kept for important men and so was translated as 'Sir'. A lady is greeted *Jambo mama*, even though *mama* means 'mother'.

After the exchange of *Jambo* you are often asked *Habari?* or *Habari gani?* This means 'News?' or 'What news?' To which the reply is always *Nzuri*, 'good', whether your news is awful or otherwise. When you knock at a door or want to enter a room, you call *Hodi!*, 'Is anyone there?' If you are welcome to enter the response is *Karibu*. Good manners would forbid you to enter without this response.

Asante and *Asante sana* mean 'thank you' and 'thank you very much'. *Sana* is a useful word to create emphasis, thus *sema sana*, 'speak up', or *kaa sana,* 'remain a long time'. As a response to a question it signifies approval, as does 'certainly' in English. 'Please' or 'If you please' is *Tafadhali*.

Pole means 'quietly' or 'slowly' and is more often used in its reduplicative form, *polepole*, when meaning slowly. *Polepole sana* would mean 'very slowly'. *Pole* is also a means of expressing sorrow, so you would say *Pole bwana* to someone who has hurt himself, or been hurt by you accidentally, or perhaps suffered a loss.

When leaving, you say *Kwa heri*, or *Kwa herini* when there are several persons.

Swahili man, Lamu

The response is the same or perhaps *Tutaonana*, 'We'll meet again!'

'Yes' is *Ndiyo* but it really means 'It is so.' Therefore remember that it can mean the opposite when in reply to a negative question such as 'Has he not arrived yet?' 'No' is *La* or *Hapana*.

Jina langu Kamau, 'My name is Kamau.' *Jina lako nani?* 'What is your name?' The pronouns are: 'I' or 'me', *Mimi;* 'you', *Wewe;* 'him/her', *Yeye;* 'us', *Sisi;* 'you' (plural), *Ninyi;* 'them', *Wao*.

Verbs

Verbs have a root that is altered by a prefix to show the person and another prefix to show the tense. Thus the verb 'speak' is *sema*, 'to speak' is *Kusema* and the person prefixes are 'I', *Ni;* 'you' *U;* 'he', *A;* 'we', *Tu;* 'you' (plural), *M;* and 'they', *Wa*. The present tense has the prefix *na*, so 'I speak' is *Ninasema* and 'we are speaking' is *Tunasema*. Some other tense prefixes are future *ta* (future), *li* (past), *me* (perfect). Thus *mlienda*, 'you (pl) went', *Amesikia*, 'He has heard', and *Tutaleta*, 'We will bring'.

Nouns

There are several classes of nouns in Swahili. Usually these are distinguished from each other by their prefix. The plural is usually different from the singular, and adjectives take different prefixes in order to agree with the class of noun that they modify. They also follow the noun. This is not the place to set out Swahili grammar, and the words or phrases used here may not be technically correct when used in other contexts. Nevertheless, you will be understood. Strictly speaking, the **numbers** are adjectives and thus will agree with the noun they modify, but the words shown below are the numbers as used with the 'N' class of nouns, the commonest.

one	*moja*	six	*sita*
two	*mbili*	seven	*aba*
three	*tatu*	eight	*nane*
four	*nne*	nine	*tisa*
five	*tano*	ten	*kumi*

'Eleven' is *Kumi na moja*, 'twelve' is *kumi na mbili*, and so on until 'twenty', which is *ishirini*. Thereafter:

thirty	*thelathini*	seventy	*sabini*
forty	*arobaini*	eighty	*themanini*
fifty	*hamsini*	ninety	*tisini*
sixty	*sitini*	hundred	*mia*

'One hundred and one' is *Mia na moja*, and so on. 'Two hundred' is *Mia mbili*, and so on to *Elfu*, 'one thousand'.

Days of the week, time, months

Saturday	*Jumamosi*	Sunday	*Jumapili*
Monday	*Jumatatu*	Tuesday	*Jumanne*
Wednesday	*Jumatano*	Thursday	*Alhamisi*
Friday	*Ijumaa*		

'A day' is *siku*, although this really means 'the time of daylight', and *usiku* is 'night-time'. *Leo* is 'today' and *kesho* 'tomorrow'. *Kesho kutwa* is 'the day after tomorrow', while *kushinda kesho kutwa* is used for the future longer than two days ahead. 'Yesterday' is *jana* and 'the other day' *juzi juzi*. 'Morning' is *asubuhi*, and *asubuhi sana* 'very early in the morning'. 'An hour' is *saa* and the time is told by counting from sunrise, so 7 am is *saa moja* and so on until *saa kumi na mbili*. To distinguish morning from evening add *asubuhi* or *jioni*. Thus 6 pm is *saa kumi na mbili jioni* and 6 am *saa kumi na mbili asubuhi*. 'Half an hour' is *nusu saa* and 'a quarter of an hour' *robo saa*. 'A minute' is *dakika*. Thus 2.20 pm is *saa nane na dakika ishirini*. *Na*, which means 'and', is used for minutes after the hour and *kasa*, which means 'less', is used for minutes before the hour. Thus 2.40 pm is *saa tisa kasa dakika ishirini*; 2.15 pm would be *saa nane na robo*; and 2.45 pm would be *saa tisa kasa robo*. 'What time is it?' is *saa ngapi*?

'A month' is *Mwezi* , and the same word also means 'moon'. The months are: *Januari, Februari, Machi, Aprili, Mei, Juni. Julai, Agosti, Septemba, Oktoba, Novemba, Desemba.*

Making Sentences

Tafadhali nilete is 'Please bring me...' 'cold water', *Maji baridi*; 'hot water', *Maji moto*; 'tea', *Chai*; 'coffee', *Kahawa*; 'milk', *Maziwa*; 'cigarettes', *Sigara*.

'Money' is *pesa*. 'How much?' is *Pesa ngapi*? and 'What is the price?' *Bei gani*? 'The price is too much for me', *Bei inanishinda*; 'reduce the price', *Punguza bei*. *Siwezi* is 'I can't' and *Hata sasa bei ni rahesi!* is 'even now the price is cheap!' With luck your request to reduce the price will elicit *Basi, nitapunguza! Nipe shillingi... tu,* which is 'Okay, I'll reduce! Give me ... shillings only.'

'What time is breakfast' (lunch, dinner)? *Chakula cha asubuhi (chakula cha ad-huhuri, chakula cha jioni), saa gani?* 'Where is the dining room?' *Chumba cha kulia ni wapi?* 'Where is the W.C.?' *Choo ni wapi?*

'Let's go!' is *Twende. Twende safari,* 'Jump in the car and let's get moving!' 'Hurry up!' is *Pesi pesi* or more politely *Pesi pesi tafadhali* . 'Slow down please' is *Nenda pole pole tafadhali.*

Signs

Some signs you may see: *Hatari,* 'Danger'; *Usiingie,* 'No entrance'; *Mbwa kali* , 'Fierce dog'; *Usinisumbue,* 'Don't disturb me'; *Kakuna kazi,* 'No jobs available'.

On T-shirts you'll see *Hakuna matata,* 'No trouble or no problem' and *Mzuri sana,* 'Very good'.

Animals

Some of the animals you are likely to see in the parks are:

antelope (roan)	*korongo*	gerenuk	*swala twiga*
antelope (sable)	*palahala*	giraffe	*twiga*
baboon	*nyani*	gnu	*nyumbu*
bat-eared fox	*mbweha masikio*	hartebeest	*kongoni*
bongo	*bongo*		(this word is
buffalo	*nyati*		now used in
bushbuck	*mbawala*		English).
bush baby	*komba*	hippopotamus	*kiboko*
cheetah	*duma*	hyena	*fisi*
crocodile	*mamba*	hyrax	*wibari*
dikdik	*dikidiki*	impala	*swala pala*
duiker	*Funo*	jackal	*mbwcha*
eland	*pofu*	klipspringer	*mbuzi mawe*
elephant	*ndovu, tembo*	kudu	*tandala*
gazelle, Thomson's	*swala tomi*	leopard	*chui*
genet cat	*kanu*	lion	*simba*

mongoose	*nguchiro*
monitor lizard	*kenge*
monkey	*kima or tumbili.*
oryx	*choroa*
reedbuck	*tohe*
rhinoceros	*kifaru*
serval cat	*mondo*
steinbuck	*dondoro*
topi	*nyahera*
warthog	*ngiri*
waterbuck	*kuro*
wild dog	*mbnyumbu*
zebra	*Punda milia*

East African brass adornments, including coiled earrings worn by Samburu and a lip plug by Turkana women (above); Masai adorning each other (right)

Recommended Reading

Geography/Ecology

Hillaby, Richard, *Journey to the Jade Sea* (Paladin, London, 1973)
Willock, Colin, *Africa's Rift Valley* (Time Life Books, Amsterdam, 1974)

Exploration

Moorehead, Alan, *The White Nile* (Penguin, London, 1967)
Pavitt, Nigel, *Kenya, The First Explorers* (Aurum Press, London, 1989)

Colonial Period

Best, Nicholas, *Happy Valley* (Secker & Warburg, London, 1979)
Blixen, Karen, *Out of Africa* (Penguin, London, 1954)
Gellhorn, Martha, *The Weather in Africa* (Eland, London, 1984)
Huxley, Elspeth, *The Flame Trees of Thika* (Penguin, London, 1962)
Markham, Beryl, *West with the Night* (Virago/Penguin, London, 1989)
Meinertzhagen, Richard, *Kenya Diary* (Eland, London, 1982)
Miller, Charles, *Battle for the Bundu* (Macdonald and Jane's, London, 1974)
Miller, Charles, *The Lunatic Express* (Westlands Sundries, Nairobi, 1987)
Perham, Margery, *East African Journey 1929–30* (Faber, London, 1976)
Roosevelt, Theodore, *African Game Trails* (Scribner's, New York, 1910)

Wildlife & Ecology

Douglas Hamilton, Iain & Oria, *Among the Elephants* (Collins/Harvill, London, 1978)
Matthiessen, Peter, *The Tree Where Man Was Born* (Picador, London, 1984)
Moss, Cynthia, *Portraits in the Wild* (University of Chicago Press, Chicago, 1975)
Myers, Norman, *The Long African Day* (Collier-McMillan, London, 1972)

Fiction

wa Thiong'o, Ngugi, *Petals of Blood* (Heinemann, London, 1986)

Guide Books

Birnie A and Noad T, *Trees of Kenya* (self-published, Kenya, 1989)
Blundell, Michael, *Wild Flowers of East Africa* (Collins, London, 1987)
Bock K R, *A Guide to Common Reef Fishes of the Western Indian Ocean* (Macmillan, London, 1978)
Haltenorth T & Diller H, *A Field Guide to the Mammals of Africa* (Collins, London, 1980)
Williams, John G, *A Field Guide to the National Parks of East Africa* (Collins, London, 1967)
—*A Field Guide to the Birds of East Africa* (Collins, London, 1980)
—*A Field Guide to the Butterflies of Africa* (Collins, London, 1969)

(following pages) *A herd of female elephants in Samburu, with their young*

Index